The
Trouble
with
Rape

The Trouble with Rape

Carolyn J. Hursch, Ph.D.

Nelson-Hall, Chicago

Library of Congress Cataloging in Publication Data

Hursch, Carolyn J.
    The trouble with rape.

    Bibliography: p.
    Includes index.
    1. Rape.   2. Rape—United States.   I. Title.
    HV6558.H87   364.1'53   76-28757
    ISBN 0-88229-323-0 (cloth)
    ISBN 0-88229-470-0 (paper)

Copyright © 1977 by Carolyn J. Hursch
Reprinted 1978

Manufactured in the United States of America.

10 9 8 7 6 5 4 3 2

Contents

Tables

Figures

Preface

The decade of the 1970s, a period of social, political, and economic upheaval, has, with its soaring crime statistics, made us aware of *rape*. And now that we are conscious of it, what next?

Is today's liberated woman more likely to encounter not only the concept, but the crime of rape? What are her reactions to rape compared with those of women of the 1960s or 1950s? Because of her more enlightened view of sex, is she better able to cope with the psychological trauma of this most personal of all crimes? Or, with an attitude toward men that sometimes verges on the vindictive, is she even more traumatized by the degradation of rape?

Has society shifted toward more compassionate treatment of the victim? Or is there still a lurking view that "Nice girls don't get raped"?

Why is rape on the increase? Why is it so difficult to prosecute? If it is such a heinous crime, why don't more women report it to the police?

Perhaps most important of all, who are the women who become rape victims? Are they different from the rest of us? And who are the rapists?

These questions and more are considered in the following pages. Some are answered in detail; for others, the results of recent research are offered so that the reader will have a basis for arriving at an answer.

While current literature is cited from the fields of criminology, psychology, psychiatry, and other disciplines, the principal contributions of this book are the results of a rape prevention research project, started in November 1973 in Denver, Colorado.

From the many sources of data available to us in conducting this study, a picture has emerged not only of the rape victim, but of the woman who successfully resists a sexual assault, and also, in shadowy outline, of the rapist himself.

My purpose in presenting these research results is to give an objective account of the facts surrounding rape, to describe the trouble spots in the legal, medical, social, and psychological handling of the problem, and to point out what should be done about the shortcomings.

The information contained in this book represents the work of many people. Data collection and analysis were painstakingly accomplished by Lou Ann Lyon and Cynthia Thomas. Nancy Hegan tracked down much of the bibliography. All three assisted in the interviewing of victims. Louise J. Leathers not only did extensive library research, but supplied encouragement. Jennie Leyba and George Garcia performed clerical work and data analysis respectively. Gertrude Martin and Kathy Von Stell were volunteer workers on the project. Dr. James Selkin was listed as codirector with me on the research grant.

The Law Enforcement Assistance Administration of the United States Department of Justice supplied funds with which to accomplish the research, as did the Denver Department of Health and Hospitals, Psychiatric Services

Division. The Denver Anti-Crime Council served as the facilitating agency, with the support of the Colorado Council of Governments.

In many ways, the greatest contribution was made by those women who informed us about the attacks they had suffered. To them this work is dedicated.

Section One:

The Facts of Rape

Chapter One

Introduction

"Rape" is the latest four-letter word in the English language to be accepted into the public vocabulary. But unlike the others which have recently been admitted to common parlance, "rape" retains its dictionary meaning—that's part of the trouble with it. Most newly emancipated four-letter words are used mainly as expletives with little or no relationship to their defined meanings. But rape is rape. And it is with exactly that meaning that it is now, still somewhat hesitantly, being pronounced out loud. For centuries it was whispered behind one's hand, not spoken in mixed company, and never mentioned in front of the children because, as everyone knew, rape wasn't nice.

We still know that. In fact, we now know, probably better than at any time in history, just how far from "nice" rape really is. And this knowledge comes to us because we have finally decided to talk about rape. In addition to those of us who are directly concerned with its prevention, the rape victim herself can now speak out about what happened to her. She can also now find the haven of a listener who will be concerned and sympathetic, and who will not forever afterward see her as a "ruined woman."

But this attitude is far from universal. It exists mainly among young women and persons of either sex who have joined the recent movements for rape prevention or victim support—a relatively small segment of society. The balance of the population accepts the present high-frequency usage of the term "rape" by the news media and the entertainment world with emotions ranging all the way from amazement through anger.

We will all hear more about rape. And it is to be hoped that any remaining reluctance to engage in open discussion of it will gradually disintegrate so that the way may be cleared for progress in dealing with it.

During the past five years, some of our inhibitions at discussing rape have been eroded away by the ever-increasing flood of articles, television shows, and lectures on this subject. At present, just about every one of the regular TV drama shows, including the new ones each fall, has now used rape as a subject of one of its episodes. Prior to that, rape was one of the most hush-hush no-no's on the air waves.

One reason for the avalanche of rape dramas now being beamed into our living rooms is that everything else that could be said about sex has already been said, photographed, and relayed to us in living color. The emancipation of rape opened up the first new subject matter for TV viewing since Neil Armstrong stepped down onto the moon.

The other reason is that rape has more impact than most topics. Everybody felt good when Armstrong's big clumsy boot slipped down into the moondust. On the other hand, the emotions aroused by a rape drama are many and varied. They include disgust, hate, fear, irritation, shame, horror, guilt, revenge, doubt—the list could go on and on, as the discussions of the shows do afterward.

Many feel that there would be no problem if rape were

not publicized; some feel that there is no such problem anyway; others are incensed by public apathy about real rapes, and many women are badly frightened as they wonder if rape could possibly happen to them.

Some of the rape dramas have erred badly and have presented situations connected with the treatment of the victim which belong in an earlier time. But, in general, the discussions, questions, and opening up of the topic are enlightening and therefore useful because, unlike the giant step of the man on the moon, each rape that occurs is a stumble backward into the Dark Ages.

Why then, has rape been a forbidden topic for so long? The obvious answer is that it concerns sex. But marriage is concerned with sex, too, and we have always been free to talk about that. Love is concerned with sex; having babies also has something to do with sex, as does the Miss America contest, fashion magazines, and yellow polka dot bikinis. Why keep rape under wraps?

The answer probably lies in the fact that the mention of rape makes us all uneasy—for different reasons depending on who we are. It makes men uneasiest of all perhaps, and usually brings forth an initial response of nervous laughter or guffaw-evoking jokes. After all, as far as the normal, but uninformed, man knows, rape is something he might suddenly do himself some night if life becomes too dull. It isn't, of course, but he knows too little about it to realize that.

On the other hand, the thoughtful normal man, after hearing the details of a forcible rape, finds it difficult to believe. He cannot imagine himself maintaining any sex drive at all when confronted by a crying, pleading woman who only complies with his wishes because of mortal fear of him. He knows that all thoughts of sex—which he equates with fun, romance, and mutual admiration—would leave him if the woman were *really* struggling to get free, especially if she were also clearly expressing repugnance for him. He does not realize that, to the rapist, the act is not "love," not ardor, and usually not even passion; it is a way of debasing and degrading a woman. (More about this later when I discuss the rapist.) Therefore, to most men, forcible rape is unreal. This gives rise to the commonly held view that: "There is no such thing as rape."

The topic makes women uneasy for a wide variety of reasons. To most women, it is almost as unreal as it is to most men because they themselves have not experienced it, and few people who have done so are in the habit of talking about it. Up until recently, most women did not even know anyone who had experienced it—or at least they were not aware that they knew a rape victim. This was because having been raped was in the same category as having had an illegitimate child or V.D.—it was a dark blot on one's character and was kept as a morbid secret.

At the same time, an occasional newspaper story about a particularly brutal rape-murder makes all women shudder. They wonder if it could possibly happen to them, and if it did, how would they react. But like all other grim possibilities that are not immediately at hand, it is much more comfortable to put the thought out of one's mind than to have it presented flatly as something that just might be lurking around the next corner regardless of how impeccable a woman's morals might be. It is the shadowy figure in the night standing over one's bed, the glimpse of a man crawling in the bedroom window, the horror of a sudden hand from nowhere clutching at one's throat. Practically every woman has, at some time, had such a nightmare. But, upon awakening, she replaces it with reproachful self-assurance: "How silly!" "Of *course* there's no one there!"

To be told that for a startlingly large number of women, the nightmare did not go away, is enlightenment that most women are happier without.

One way of coping with such knowledge is to imagine, and then believe, that women to whom rape happens are in some way vastly different from oneself. Deciding that they must have been taller, shorter, fatter, thinner, older, or younger will not work since rape victims come in all variations of these attributes. It is far easier to settle on some impalpable quality which is not so easily measured with a ruler or scale. This accounts for the overwhelming number of women who firmly believe that most claims of being raped are either outright lies, or that the rapes were brought on by the victim herself, who was "out looking for it."

In the majority of rapes, if the actual details of each assault were made public, it would quickly dispel these views. But rape details seldom are made public. The mores of news reporting do not allow it. In one sense, this is just as well because the full reporting of all the details might cause a change in the American way of life—few people could stand complete rape stories with their morning coffee.

It takes a strong stomach and repeated exposure to become habituated to the details of what actually happens to rape victims. During and after a war, we often read of the tortures inflicted on prisoners of war. Such things as being forced to drink one's own urine or being made to kneel on a stone floor for several hours are undeniably shocking, painful, and degrading. But they are part of the horrors of war, and with war's end, we rejoice that no one in *our* civilization will again be forced to endure such indignities. Returning prisoners of war are treated with awe and respect because of having lived through such humiliation and suffering.

Yet, every night of the year (statistically speaking, once every fourteen minutes day and night, all year long) here in our civilized society, some woman endures treatment which is every bit as horrible, just as degrading, and equally painful. Being stripped naked by two men, and held flat on one's back among the trash cans in an alley by one of them, while the other repeatedly rams a dirty Coke bottle from one of those trash cans into one's vagina is not very civilized. But no one lauds the victim for surviving. No one invites her to the White House for dinner in honor of what she has had to live through.

We cringe at the thought of small children in wartime

being neglected, hungry, or shot at. Yet, at least one out of every five rape victims in this country is under twelve years of age, and many are as young as four or five years old. Their scars are as deep as the war orphan's, but their stories can never be told. The public cannot reach out to them with sympathy and understanding for what they have been through. Instead, they are often severely scolded by a parent, or at the very least they must be admonished to never mention the incident again. If it should become known, neighbors who used to be close friends, will not allow their children to play with a little girl who has been raped.

So, rape has flourished and increased, like a hidden infestation, because it is hard to face. Therefore, the first step in reversing this trend must be to examine the facts. After that, the fiction must be sheared away and discarded. Then the social climate surrounding the rape victim must be considered, as well as the propensities of the public and private agencies who take up her cause and the motivations of the rapist. Only then will it be clear what steps must be taken in order to clear up the trouble with rape.

Chapter Two

Researching Rape

To launch a study of rape and its victims in the Denver area, my co-workers and I appealed to the local media to publicize our need for volunteers who had been rape victims. In general, we wanted to find out where, when, and to whom such attacks had occurred. In addition, one of our specific questions was "How do women who successfully ward off such attacks go about doing it?" Therefore, we needed detailed information from women who had actually been raped, as well as from women who had faced a rapist alone, and had succeeded in thwarting his purpose.

We received immediate cooperation from newspapers and radio and TV personnel in the area. In fact, with the news of our being funded to conduct the project, many came to us and offered all possible assistance. They freely publicized our need for "victims" and "resisters."

We offered no inducements to these women to tell us their story, except the opportunity to participate in a scientific study which might, some day, help other victims. But we did assure them that their names would never be used. To make certain of this, we never asked for a full name. Instead, we only asked them what they wanted us to call them—Sue, Mary, Jane—and this name was immediately assigned a number. To this day, many of our victims remain unidentified even to us; we know them only as Karen, No. 109; Ruth, No. 110, and so on. Others, after the interview, offered their services to us free to be used in any way that might help with our project. These people volunteered complete names and addresses, and many later became close friends and associates.

In all cases, they gave their time to tell us their stories and answer our questions, which usually took a minimum of two hours. What we learned from these interviews is discussed in this first section.

In planning the study, we felt that it would probably be quite easy to get the stories of rape resisters, but perhaps difficult to convince actual rape victims to come in and be interviewed. But we were wrong. Many rape victims responded to the call. Once the interview was begun, they became at ease and not only told us all we asked for, but many offered a great deal of additional, useful information. Some were still tense and anxiety-ridden because of their experience; some were depressed and bitter about it; all were keenly interested in doing anything they could to help reduce the crime of rape and its aftermath.

They came from all walks of life. Some had had unfortunate family patterns and had been raped as small children. Others were suburban housewives, raped on a calm morning when the peacefulness of their existence made them negligent about locking the back door as they went about their housework. Many were young, in their early twenties, wearing the long, straight hair which places them in this generation. They had all been deeply hurt— some with severe physical wounds that took months to heal—but all with aching psychological bruises, some of which they would wear forever.

To our surprise, few rape resisters came. We later learned that this was not because there were few to come. They hesitated because the experience is so common that many women felt that what had happened to them would not be "important enough" for us to record. Many phoned, almost apologetically, explaining that they did not know whether or not we would be interested in their story. They would then proceed to describe a threatening encounter from which they had fought or talked their way free. We were, of course, keenly interested.

It gradually became apparent that many, many women had extricated themselves from such situations, but if a woman had escaped with little physical harm before the sex act took place, she simply breathed a huge sigh of relief, went on her way, and more or less repressed the incident— much as one tends to toss off a "close one" when driving an automobile. Our public lectures on rape often reminded these women of the frightening incident. But, in the context of open discussions of the horror of an actual rape, women who had narrowly escaped it felt that their experience had been trivial by comparison.

However, since theirs were the success stories of rape, we were anxious to hear them and gradually were able to convince enough of them to come in for complete interviews. The methods they had used to avoid rape will be discussed in detail later.

Additional data on rape and all other sexual assaults was obtained through the cooperation of the Denver Police Department. They turned over to us their complete file of sex offenses for the year 1973 after having the victim's names deleted from the reports. This amounted to 1,045 offense reports, which allowed us to tabulate demographic information on victims, resisters, and sex offenders. These tabulations are shown in succeeding chapters.

Information was also made available to us by the Emergency Room of Denver General Hospital regarding the 336 rape victims admitted there during 1973, and by the

Denver Visiting Nurse Service who offered aid to these victims in their homes shortly after the rape.

Long before we had worked our way through this mountain of information, it was apparent that here was a lost pocket of misfortune full of unbelievable neglect, despair, and trouble.

Chapter Three

Who Gets Raped

The 1,045 sex offenses reported to the Denver police during 1973 involved a total of 1,150 victims. In some cases there was more than one victim. There were, for example, a few cases where a group of men kidnapped and then passed around one or two women. There were also cases of indecent exposure to a group of two or three small girls, and other such instances.

We grouped all of the sex offenses under six categories:

1. Rape of a woman age 16 or over
2. Rape of a girl under age 16
3. Attempted rape of a woman age 16 or over
4. Child molestation other than rape
5. Sexual assault, other than rape, on an adult woman
6. Sexual assault on a male victim of any age

For groups 1 through 5, age sixteen was used as the

dividing line in order to coincide with the legal definition of statutory rape in Colorado which existed during the period of the study. Child molestation, category 4, was separated from Rape under 16, category 2, because rape is obviously the more serious crime, and we wanted to know the extent of it as opposed to the less traumatic forms of sexual molestation to a child.

Category 5, Sexual assault other than rape, includes indecent exposure, voyeurism, indecent liberties, obscene telephone calls, or any combination of these offenses. Male victims, category 6 were all grouped together since this constitutes a slightly different type of crime with a different motivation on the part of the perpetrator. However, most of the victims in this group were young boys. (See Table 1.)

Table 1
False Reports* and Sex Offense Categories

Sex Offense Category	Number of Actual Victims	Number of False Reports	% of False Reports in Category	Total "Victims" Reporting
1 Rape, 16 and over	291	14	.04	305
2 Rape, under 16	69	4	.05	73
3 Attempted rape	162	5	.03	167
4 Child molestation	179	12	.06	191
5 Sexual assault	351	7	.02	358
6 Male victims	56	0	0	56
TOTALS	1108	42	.04	1150

*False reports are those cases in which the "victim" admitted she was lying, or where the police for other reasons decided that she was lying. See Table 19 in Chapter 9 for details. (From Denver Police Sex Offense Reports for 1973)

There were 370 cases of rape and 165 cases of attempted rape reported to the Denver police in 1973. Of these, 262 went to the city hospital (Denver General) for examination or treatment, or both, after the assault. However, an additional seventy-four rape victims came to Denver General Hospital who never reported the crime to the police. Other victims went to one of the many private hospitals in the area. Some went to their own doctors; some received no medical attention at all.

Some of the reasons behind violent crimes may lie in ethnic tensions. Also, one ethnic group may be more highly victimized than other groups because of distinctive ethnic characteristics. Therefore, we were interested in knowing which groups our victims came from, and whether or not the victim population had the same ethnic makeup as the citizen population of Denver. Obviously if one group is more highly represented in the victim population than it is in the general population, then we might conclude that ethnic background had something to do with being selected as a victim.

At the same time, extreme caution must be applied in arriving at such conclusions since ethnic background may not be the primary factor. Instead, it may be contingent on a more relevant factor such as geographic location. For example, if Ethnic Group A tends to be concentrated in one low-rent section of the city, and this same section is easily accessible to transients and indigents who depend for their existence on charity and petty thievery, then Ethnic Group A will bear the brunt of such crimes in that area. But the determining factor will be location, not ethnic group, since any ethnic group living there would receive the same treatment.

Therefore, in considering the implications of one ethnic group standing out over another, either as victims or as offenders, all of the attending factors need to be analyzed. Some of these, such as income level, religious practices, social habits, family life, and geographic location may be much more important than the ethnicity itself.

Table 2
Ethnic Backgrounds of Sex Assault Victims

Sex Offense Categories	Anglo	Black	Chicano	Other
1—Rape, 16 and over	76.8	10.8	11.8	0.7
2—Rape, under 16	58.6	22.8	18.6	0.0
3—Attempted rape	78.5	7.0	13.3	1.3
Subtotal— Categories 1, 2 & 3	74.8	11.2	13.1	0.8
4—Child molestation	76.3	8.6	15.0	0.0
5—Sexual assault	81.6	8.4	9.6	0.3
6—Male victims	75.9	13.0	11.1	0.0
Victim percentages— All categories	77.2	10.0	12.3	0.5
Denver area percentages*	72.7	9.1	16.6	1.6

*Source—*Selected Census Statistics Totaled for each Denver Councilmanic District and for the City and County of Denver.* Denver Department of Health and Hospitals. September 1972.

With that warning, I present Table 2. The first row of data in the table shows that 76.8 percent of the rape victims of age sixteen and older are Anglos. This contrasts with 72.7 percent Anglos (see last row of figures in table) in the Denver population. Thus, there is a slightly higher percentage of Anglo victims than Anglo citizens in Denver. Black victims constitute 10.8 percent of the total, which is very close to the 9.1 percent of blacks in the Denver population.

Chicano victims constitute only 11.8 percent of the rape victims, whereas they account for 16.6 percent of the Denver population. This is a surprisingly low percentage of the victim population especially since much of the Chicano population in Denver is concentrated in the downtown districts where crime rates are generally high.

Here we must consider other factors. Many Chicano families are devoutly religious. The older and more restrictive religions have always had a problem in dealing with rape victims. Regardless of the woman's lack of complicity in the crime, she is still impure after being raped. She is no longer virginal, and the man who marries her must be content with receiving "damaged goods." Therefore, a highly religious culture and/or a culture which puts severe restrictions on the individual, tends to bury the crime of rape. Its victims are clothed in shame forever; therefore no public outcry is possible for them. Women in such a culture would be inhibited from reporting a rape and making it a matter of public record.

In this context, an article by A. F. Schiff (see bibliography), states that in attempting to determine rape rates in several countries in Europe, "Spain, even with an assist from the security officer at the American Embassy, was the most reluctant to give information." And again, "One authority in Rome did concede that the incidence of sexual assault was high, but that the crime was greatly under-reported since it was considered a great disgrace to have been raped."

Also, within many cultures, there is a strong sense of machismo, which dictates that such matters are not only kept within the family, but are also avenged by male members of the family. This too, would lead to under-reporting.

In short, it seems quite likely that the 11.8 percent of Chicano rapes shown in Table 2 may reflect under-reporting of the crime by that ethnic group.

At the same time, the second row of Table 2 which shows rapes of children under sixteen years of age, seems to present a paradox to the above. In this tabulation, rapes of black children constitute 22.5 percent of all child rapes. This is more than twice what would be expected from the 9.1 percent of black representation in the Denver population. Also, rapes of Chicano children account for 18.3 percent of the total, as contrasted with only 16.6 percent Chicanos in the population. This is a drastic increase for both minority groups over the reported adult rape rate.

This vast difference in the percent of minority adult rapes reported and the percent of minority child rapes reported may reflect another social factor: distrust of the prevailing white Anglo "establishment" by the minorities. One of the troubles with rape is that a victim who reports it must always be ready to face the suspicion that she was not really raped at all, or that she encouraged the man to think that she wanted him to rape her. A victim must feel very certain, not only of her innocence, but also of her ability to prove it, in order to summon up enough courage to pick up the phone and call in the predominantly white law enforcement personnel. An overweight of religious taboo or a social history or distrust of these personnel—or both—would effectively deter a victim from following that course.

However, the whole matter of child rape is a different story. To begin with, society's indignation at a hurt to any child is great. It is one of the few areas where race, creed, and color come close to being truly ignored. A parent's remorse—any parent's—at the violation of his child is shared by all parents. Therefore, the reporting, which is done, of course, by the parent or guardian, carries less risk since the parent is not crying out because of his own hurt but because of that of his child. With an adult rape, the report must be made by the adult; and it is always more difficult to make one's own case than it is to make a case for one's child.

The second factor is perhaps even more important. In the adult case, it is necessary to show that the woman did not give her consent to the sexual act. This is not necessary in the case of a child. Statutory rape in Colorado (at the time of this study) was defined as sexual intercourse with a minor (that is, a female under age sixteen) by a person at least two years older than the minor. Whether or not the minor gave her consent to this act is irrelevant; it is still statutory rape with or without consent. Apparently the law considers a child under sixteen as incapable of judging whether or not she should engage in the act. Thus, this cloudy factor is removed from the problem and a report of intercourse under these conditions is statutory rape with no need to prove who initiated the act, or whether or not the child agreed to it.

Therefore, reporting a child rape is far easier than reporting an adult rape. Prosecution is another matter because few children make good witnesses in a court trial. And, in this state, as well as many others, the child will be questioned on the witness stand if the case is prosecuted. But Table 2 lists only the reporting of rape regardless of the disposition of the case. Table 24 displays the number and type of cases which go to court, and the reasons why many do not.

The rate of sexual offenses increases in the warm months, and seems to hit a yearly low in late fall and early winter, with December generally showing the lowest rate.

This seasonal variation has been noted by many sociologically-oriented authors and practically all law enforcement personnel. It was even given an imposing name as far back as 1869 when Adolphe Quetelet announced his "thermic law of delinquency." This resulted from his observations that there is more crime in warm countries than in cold countries, and more in warm seasons than in cold seasons. Many writers since then have pondered this "law" and expressed various philosophical theories relating to it. However, in the case of sexual assaults, there seems to be little mystery as to why they should be more prevalent in good weather, and there hardly seems to be any need for abstruse theory to explain it. The rapist feels the cold just like anyone else. A back alley filled with slush and ice is hardly the place to linger, much less to take off one's clothes and get down on the ground. The same is true of crawling in windows, most of which will be closed and locked during cold weather. Nor are there many women

Table 3

Sex Offenses Reported to Denver Police in 1973

Months	Rape—16 and over	Rape under 16	Attempted Rape	Total rapes and attempted rapes	Child molestation	Sexual assault	Male victims	Totals all categories
January	25	5	13	43	10	31	3	87
February	14	10	13	37	10	25	3	75
March	18	7	9	34	11	27	6	78
April	25	8	12	45	15	25	4	89
May	19	10	11	40	7	23	5	75
June	33	6	11	50	18	49	1	118
July	36	9	16	61	10	25	3	99
August	35	3	24	62	18	43	11	134
September	37	6	12	55	7	19	0	81
October	20	5	17	42	12	34	1	89
November	20	3	9	32	15	17	4	68
December	18	1	14	33	8	9	2	52
TOTAL	300	73	161	534	141	327	43	1,045

strolling along the streets wearing light clothing which can be easily ripped off. Tearing away a ski parka, pants, and overshoes before he even gets close to his objective may take considerably longer than the assailant can afford to spend on preliminaries.

In other words, it hardly seems necessary to postulate that a natural biological tide surges higher in the human animal in warm than in cold months, when it is apparent that the inconveniences caused by the low temperatures and bad weather itself would curtail this activity just as they do many other activities, such as kite flying, touch football, and outdoor barbecues.

Table 4

Sex Assaults on Women Age 45 and Older

Sex Offense Category	Number	% of Category
Rape (Age range 45-74)	18*	5.0
Attempted rape (Age range 45-72)	4	2.4
Sexual assault (Age range 45-86)	23	6.4
Total	45	5.0

*Three of these were not represented in the Denver Police Sex Offense Reports, but were obtained from Denver General Hospital Emergency Room data. (Data from Denver Police Sex Offense Reports for 1973)

The average age of adult rape victims who reported the crime to the Denver Police in 1973 was 24.3 years. The average age for all types of sexual assaults was 21.4 years.

While most of the victims were between the ages of 16 and 34, attacks were made on women of all ages from very young to very old. Table 4 shows the number of assaults and the age range in each category made upon women of age 45 and older. These constituted a total of 5 percent of all adult rapes, and 6.5 percent of all sexual assaults (other than rape) committed on adults. Note that the age range for the actual rapes went up to 74, and the age range for other types of sexual assaults went to age 86.

Despite the fact that it has often been observed that "rape is a young man's crime," there is obviously no upper limit on the age of the victims of these crimes. It will also be apparent in later tables, that there is hardly any lower limit either since every year some victims are very young children.

The problem of child rape and sexual molestation of children is one which no one likes to dwell on. Apparently, this is true because so little can be done about it by public agencies before it happens, and the problem of erasing the trauma of it afterwards is not easy either.

But child rape does occur, and with an alarming frequency. We found that 24.5 percent of all sexual assaults by adults were committed on children. This includes victims of both sexes, with "children" defined as persons under age sixteen. We found that 23.3 percent of actual rapes were committed on female children. Table 5 shows the number of child sex assaults for 1973 which were either reported to the Denver Police or where the children were brought to Denver General Hospital for treatment after the assault, or both. Table 5 also shows the breakdown into ethnic backgrounds for these children and indicates the percentage of the total that they represent in each ethnic group. Note that eleven of these 295 sexual offenses committed on children were brought to the hospital for treatment but were not reported to the police.

Table 5 shows that for the year 1973, 24 percent of sexual offenses to Anglos were committed on child victims, 30.2 percent of black victims were children, and 35.1 percent of Chicano victims were children.

Some of the offenses indicated in Table 5 are relatively minor, such as an obscene telephone call or a brief indecent exposure. Therefore, Table 6 separates out the actual rapes,

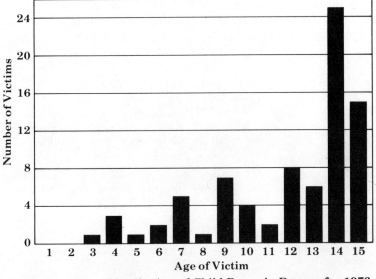

Figure 1. Age Distribution of Child Rapes in Denver for 1973.

With regard to rapes and other sexual assaults on children, these figures must be regarded as simply the tip of the iceberg. Rape is said to be the most unreported crime, and while there are many reasons which keep adults from reporting it, there are many more which keep the child from doing so. A four- or five-year-old can hardly walk into the police station and report that she has been raped. She would probably not be listened to on the phone even if she knew the appropriate action to take or agency to call. Often a child will attempt to tell a parent or guardian about such an event, only to be silenced because the child's story seems preposterous. The truth of the report may be picked up later by a schoolteacher.

It has been generally assumed by professionals who work with children that child rape and sexual molestation are largely a matter of incest. While a great deal of incest may occur and go unreported, we found that 50 percent of the reported cases of child rape were committed by total strangers. This is shown in Table 7, which shows that another 35.7 percent of child rapes were committed by persons known to the child, but not related to her.

Table 7

Relationship of Child Victim to Offender
(False Reports Excluded)

Category	Attacks by relative No.	% of Category	Attacks by Person Known (but not related) to Victim No.	% of Category	Attacks by Stranger No.	% of Category
Rape of a female under 16	10	14.3	25	35.7	35	50.0
Sexual molestation (other than rape) female under 16	5	2.8	33	18.2	143	79.0
Sexual molestation male under 16	1	3.0	5	15.2	27	81.8

(Data from Denver Police Department Sex Offense Reports for 1973)

Under "sexual molestation" in the other two categories on Tables 7 and 8, we have included all attacks which did not result in an actual rape. Some of these obviously did not have rape as the intent since they were indecent exposures where the offender disappeared of his own accord after exposing himself. Here, too, the greatest proportion of these offenses reported were committed by persons who were strangers to the child—79 percent for sexual molestation to female children and 81.8 percent of the sexual molestations to male children. Only a small percentage of the sexual molestations were committed by family members—2.8 percent to females, and 3 percent to males.

It should be emphasized that these are all offenses which were reported to the police. In many cases of this type

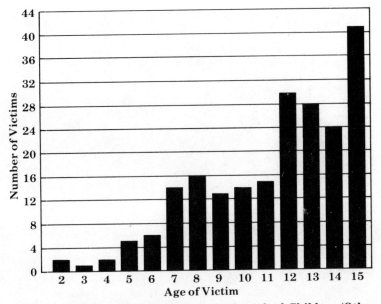

Figure 2. Age Distribution of Sexually Assaulted Children (Other than Rape Victims) in Denver for 1973.

which occur within the family, no report is made to police because of the resulting disgrace to the entire family. This is also true many times when the attacker is not related, but known to the child as a neighbor, or a close friend of an adult member of the family. The desire not to ruin the life of the close friend may prevent the family of the child from reporting the offense—although the incident may end the friendship. Sometimes retribution for the harm done to the child is carried out by her family rather than bringing the matter to the attention of police. Sometimes the child will later confide the experience to a schoolteacher or other counselor, but many such incidents are never brought to light until the child reaches adulthood and seeks help for a resultant problem.

Table 8

Relatives and Persons Known to Victims (False Reports Excluded)

Category	Attacks by Relative								Attacks by Person Known to (but not Related to) Victim				
	Father	Brother	Cousin	Half Brother	Uncle	Step Father	Brother-in-law	Step Uncle	Mother's Boyfriend	Other
Rape female under 16	5	1	1	1	2	0	1	0	2	22
Sexual molestation (other than rape) female under 16	5	0	0	0	0	3	0	2	1	27
Sexual molestation male under 16	0	0	0	0	1	0	0	0	0	5

(Data from Denver Police Department Sex Offense Reports for 1973)

Table 8 breaks down the attacks by family members and other known persons according to the exact relationship.

The figures in Tables 7 and 8 probably represent the top of an iceberg because so many of these attacks are not reported. But, they do make it clear that whatever unreported abuse of a sexual nature the child faces within her home environment, there is also a great deal more waiting for her out on the street.

Much attention has been paid recently to child abuse in the form of cruel and unusual punishment, neglect, and malnutrition. Agencies have been set up in many cities to investigate and deal with these problems. Such help has usually been spurred by tragic cases of physically battered children who are brought into city hospitals with bruises and wounds from suspicious causes.

However, because of the nature of the sex attack and the resultant implications both for the child and the offender, child rape and molestation cases are never publicized. Therefore, few people are aware of the extent of this crime. And, while it is obviously just as prevalent as other forms of child abuse, there are few facilities for handling it.

Since the prognosis for normal sexual adjustment as an adult is poor for the untreated child rape victim, the above figures are alarming. Certainly child abuse legislation and funding should be expanded to cover those cases where incest is practiced on the child, and where a child is attacked by a stranger and will need extensive therapy in order to achieve normal adulthood.

Despite the harm done, the offenders in these child cases are rarely prosecuted. The problem here is that few small children make good witnesses in court. Unless the evidence was obtained immediately after the rape by a careful medico-legal expert and unless such evidence is overwhelming, there is little chance of successfully prosecuting the offender. The child may be too frightened on the witness stand to state the details correctly many months afterward, and her statements can easily be distorted by cross-examination. The law that requires a child to go through this procedure seems badly in need of change. It is distressing enough for an adult to take the witness stand, and to be cross-examined by an ardent defense attorney. The whole process could be to the child, as it is to many adult victims, almost as traumatic as the rape itself.

Chapter Four

Where Rapes Occur

Rape is primarily an inner city crime, yet in some forms it spreads out to suburban areas. Other sex offenses have no geographical boundaries.

We found that out of 125 census tracts in Denver, six tracts in the downtown area accounted for one-third of the adult rapes. This was not true for child rape and molestation, which was distributed throughout the city and its suburbs.

Other high rape areas include districts which have a high concentration of multi-level apartment buildings, city parks, college and university campuses and their adjacent streets, and any outlying districts where there are groups of small cut-rate stores, bars, pawn shops, and older buildings.

Unlike the burglar who ranges into the upper middle-class suburban neighborhoods in order to make his break-in as profitable as possible with silver items and expensive jewelry, the rapist rarely approaches such homes. The exception to this is the occasional carefully planned entry by an itinerant in the area, who waits for the husband's car to leave the driveway, then makes his entrance when he is fairly certain that the woman is alone and attending to household chores. Mid-morning is a rather peaceful time in such neighborhoods, with children away at school. A woman may be doing her laundry in the basement, with no concern about having left her backdoor open or unlocked so that her neighbor may dash in for coffee. The practice may have been observed by a burglar or rapist, or may be stumbled on fortuitously by a transient workman with a penchant for rape.

The professional thief rarely wastes his time on sexual assaults while plying his trade. His profits are built on his ability to get in and out of a house quickly without being seen. An excellent life history of such a professional is contained in the book *Are You Safe from Burglars* by Robert Earl Barnes (Pocket Books, New York, 1973). Writing the book from prison, Barnes frankly discusses all aspects of his profession, and he also includes many tips on making one's premises burglar-proof. These tips also apply, of course, to keeping out rapists. While the break-in rape is not a large problem in suburban homes, it can and does occur. Also, while *most* burglars will not take time out to rape while committing a theft, there is no guarantee of this.

More than half of all rapes occur in homes, most of which are apartments located in the metropolitan areas. The others take place in alleys, parks, open fields, and cars. The use of an automobile is essential to many rapes, especially the gang rape. Therefore, heavily traveled, business-lined highways leading out of town are frequently the hunting grounds of the rapist. A lone woman waiting at a bus stop at night on such a highway is a likely target. Most traffic is moving at a rapid pace, and such areas contain few private homes since the homes are tucked away on the quieter side streets. Therefore, since most of the businesses are closed, the occupants of cars are hurrying toward somewhere else. A fleeting glimpse of people struggling beside an open car door is not enough to cause a driver to stop the flow of traffic while he tries to cross over to investigate. Even a scream will not register much on other drivers since it will be muffled by the sounds of traffic and car radios.

Child molestation and child rape have a wide, unlimited geographic range, although there is some concentration in the neighborhood of schools. In many cases, the child is picked up on her way to or from school, then transported some distance away. In all districts, regardless of the affluence or poverty of the neighborhood, there are "cruisers" circling the schools in the afternoon at the time the children start for home. Some of these are exhibitionists only; others are rapists. Some will cruise for many afternoons before selecting a particular child; others are looking for any child walking alone.

If no lone child is discovered, then various devices are used to cut one child out of the crowd, particularly if the target is younger children. For example, one habitual offender raped a number of children in the six- to eight-year-old range by using the following ruse to isolate his victim: Seeing a group of three or four children, he would pull his car to the curb around a corner ahead of them, get out, and appear to be looking around. When they approached him, he would inquire as to whether or not they had seen a black and white puppy running loose. They would reply that they had not, but the problem caught their interest. He then explained that his puppy had run off, and that he must find it immediately before it got run over since it had never been out alone before.

Nearly all children will respond to this kind of come-on. Most of them are wary these days about a man offering them candy to get in his car. If their parents have not emphasized this warning, their sophistication about cavities in their teeth will prompt them to refuse the candy anyway. But a lost puppy goes right to a child's heart.

They were always eager to help him find it. Obviously,

speed was essential since any moment lost might mean that the mythical puppy would be run over. The man then suggested that "you three boys go look over in that area, and this girl and I will look down this street." Everybody followed his commands and he was able to lead his victim right into his car around the corner.

He would then speed away to a distant part of town, rape the girl, and drop her off in a remote area near a shopping center where she could find help in getting home. Usually the child had no idea of where she had been taken. The flaw in this whole process was in not bargaining on a child's ability to recall small details, and this rapist was finally caught by the detailed description given by several of his victims of small peculiarities of the inside of his car. Unlike an adult, they were unable to tell the make of the car, but their color descriptions were more accurate than an adult's might be, and other features, such as the dashboard, windshield, and upholstery, were amazingly accurate.

Ten- and eleven-year-olds, emulating their older sisters by standing at the curb with their thumbs extended after school, are prime targets. There is no risk at all in stopping and picking them up since many parents are pulling up to the curb and collecting their offspring for the day. No one will even notice.

Some of these cruisers will take the girl into the car, expose themselves to her or masturbate in front of her, then let her out. Others will rape her. Young boys are also picked up in this way and either touched or fondled by the offender, then released, or forced into participating in a sexual act. Occasionally, children of both sexes are murdered in this type of situation after being sexually molested.

Older victims of rape and other sexual assaults are usually attacked in their homes. The offender either breaks in while the victim is sleeping, or comes to her door and gains entrance on some pretext, or simply forces his way past the victim once she has opened the door. Such rapes are

Chapter Five

Who Rapes

Any generalization of the rapist, or sex offender, is at this point premature. Programs for the treatment of rapists are fairly rare, and new. Most research reports to date include only a few cases, from which it is dangerous to come to conclusions about rapists in general.

Traditionally, rapists have been sentenced to prison for varying numbers of years to pay for their crime, rather than to treatment centers for whatever flaws in their characters, personality, or psychological makeup caused them to commit rape.

Psychological and criminal theory traditionally has held that each type of offender sticks to his own peculiar type of offense, and that a Peeping Tom need not be feared since he will only peep, an exhibitionist will only exhibit, a "toucher" (one who reaches under a woman's dress or in some other way furtively touches her body) will only "touch." However, we now know that this theory is not true.

The history of many sex offenders shows that they may

engage in various types of sex offenses along the way, with the more innocuous types preceding actual rape. For example, there may have been a complaint from a neighbor in the man's early teens, that he had made crude sexual advances toward her young daughter, then a charge of voyeurism (the Peeping Tom) in mid-teens, somewhat later a simple assault on a mature woman, then a series of rapes. In these cases, it is as though what seemed like early teenage pranks, have gradually developed into rape.

In other cases, a man may actually engage in voyeurism regularly all his life, until he is in his late fifties or sixties. Sometimes such men are caught, charged, given a penalty, after which they move to another town and go on peeping. These cases do follow the old dictum—they never do any more than peek in windows.

But it is clear now that it is impossible to predict without a great deal of other information whether any given sex offender will progress to more violent sex crimes, or merely continue throughout his life with the offense he is committing. Some do, some do not.

In this connection, the autobiography of Lance Rentzel gives an enlightening view of one type of sex offender, the exhibitionist. The book is entitled *When All the Laughter Died in Sorrow* (New York: Bantam Books, 1973). In this case, the exhibitionist did no harm whatsoever to his victims, other than whatever psychological impact there is for a young girl in experiencing the exposures. There was no progression to greater crimes. Also, the exhibitionism occurred only twice during adulthood, with a long span of years in between. Other exhibitionists may expose themselves ten or fifteen times a week, every week, year after year. Still others may do so as a prelude to a rape later on that same evening.

A few familiar "types" of rapists will be discussed here, as they are encountered in police reports and other purely factual accounts. But no attempt will be made to delve into the psychological processes which cast these men into these modes of behavior. There are many other sexual offenders who do not fit into these type castings at all. It will take much more research and treatment experience to set up any meaningful classification of types. However, the following are descriptions of rapists who have been apprehended.

Rapist A is nineteen years old, white, and fairly intelligent. He left high school as soon as the law permitted him to. He had never had any close friends of either sex. As a child he had lived with several different relatives, one after the other, since first one then the other of his own parents had died. He was a troublesome child in many small ways, and had never done well in school. He had a few minor scrapes with the law in his early teens, once for stealing women's underthings from a clothesline, once for joy-riding. He had had one low-paying job after another, none of which worked out well, nor had any future promise. He was given to fits of temper, excessive drinking, and moodiness. Shortly after a job which he had hopes of getting was awarded to someone else, he raped a young woman about his own age in his own neighborhood, although he and she were strangers. He raped four more women in the same neighborhood before he was arrested at his home one morning, wearing the same distinctive clothing he wore during each of the rapes. None of the women was badly hurt, but he had overpowered each and threatened them with a knife.

Rapist B's story is similar except that he is twenty-eight years old and has been married twice. Each of his marriages broke up, the second one just a few weeks before he started raping women. In each marriage, he was not only dominated by his wife but frequently belittled by her, according to his account. It was much like his childhood where he was frequently belittled by an otherwise doting mother and an older sister. Rapist B also had little success in school, few friends of either sex, and many menial, low-paying jobs. He assaulted nine women who reported it to the police before he was caught. All of them were between twenty and twenty-two years old, and all were strangers to him. All of his rapes were committed by gaining entrance to an apartment in the daytime where there was a woman home alone. Most of these women were married and did not work away from home. He told each the same story when he appeared at their door—that he had come a long distance on a bicycle to see someone in a nearby apartment and now found no one at home. He asked to use the telephone. He overpowered each of the women after he had gained entrance to the apartment, by grabbing them from behind, and pressing a pair of scissors into their ribs. Four of these women were able to talk him out of raping them by various ruses. The other five he raped.

Rapist B took great care to remove possible fingerprints he might have left in each apartment, remembering to wipe any glass or metal object he touched. He gave each woman a false name by which to call him, the same name every time. He warned each not to report the incident to the police since, "I've killed five women already, and I'll come back and kill you." (This, so far as police were able to determine later, was not true.) He was caught because of his car, which he parked in an alley beside the apartment building of one of his victims. Since this rape (like all of his others) had occurred in broad daylight, the victim saw him (as several other victims had) go out and get into his car afterward. However, this time the car did not start, so the offender got out again and walked away, leaving the car in the alley. The victim notified the police of the rape and pointed out the car to them. When Rapist B came back the following day with a tow truck to haul his car away, police arrested him.

The above story illustrates the strange mixture of caution and negligence that characterizes the behavior of many offenders. While fingerprints were carefully wiped off the glass he used, he returned to pick up an old, worthless car with a tow truck in broad daylight.

Rapist C is in prison for life. He was convicted of rape-murder after killing nine women over a period of a few years. He is large, strong, and good looking. He freely states that he does not belong in society and would be fearful of being released from prison. Recently, when asked what he would do now if he were free and started to rape a woman who tried to physically resist him, he immediately answered that he would kill her. His history bears this out. He raped many women over a period of time and enjoyed hearing them plead with him, cry, moan, and curse him. But if they attempted to get away or to physically fight him in any way, something snapped inside him, and the woman ended up strangled. He did not consciously decide to kill them; it just happened, as though he were programmed to do it. He knows now that he has no control over this impulse after a certain point and feels secure in prison because he will not kill women there.

Some common attitudes do exist among rapists. One of these is that it is important to dehumanize the woman, to keep her anonymous and to see her as an object rather than as a person.

Rapist D is twenty-four years old and is about to be released from prison. He was sent there for three years after severely beating a woman on the street. He admits that he had previously raped a number of women most of whom he did not know, but they either did not report it or did not give a good enough description of him for the police to arrest him for it. He has been in many bar and street fights with other men, and in his early teens, he spent some time in a reformatory for severely injuring another boy in a fight. He is not sure that he will not return to raping women when he gets out of prison. He feels that if everything goes all right, and he has enough money for everything he wants to buy, and plenty of good, close friends, he may not. But if things don't go well, he doesn't know what will happen, and he is somewhat afraid to think too much about it.

He is angry about his childhood, his parents, and the poor life they lived. He admits that they probably gave him all they could under the circumstances, but he has many petty grievances against them, such as the fact that his older sister and brother seemed to get more of everything than he did. He is angry at the school system which didn't teach him anything useful, and the teachers who got good pay for doing so little. He is angry at people who own fast, powerful cars, and he feels they all live dishonest lives in order to make money enough to buy them.

He was married once for nearly a year, but his wife earned more on her job than he did on his, and he was finally fired, thereby making her the sole breadwinner. During the time he was out of work, he would frequently go "looking for broads" with a friend, and once was charged by a neighbor woman of harassing her because he tossed lewd remarks at her as she walked by his house. On another occasion he was almost caught by the police. He had hidden behind a fence and was blowing birdshot at the buttocks of any woman who walked by. He saw the police car coming around the corner just in time to get away. He counts the days and hours until he will be released from prison, but gets more nervous about how he will make out on the outside, with every day that passes.

So far we have been describing lone rapists. An equally frightening and usually more sadistic phenomenon is the gang rape, which is defined here as a situation involving more offenders than victims. In our study of sex assaults in Denver for 1973, we found that there were fifty-seven gang rapes and sixteen attempted gang rapes. Of the fifty-seven gang rapes, eleven were committed on females under age sixteen. Table 12 shows the occurrence, by month, of these gang rapes and attempted rapes, as well as all other sexual offenses committed by gangs.

The seasonal variation of lone rapes is seen also in these gang assaults, which are largely a phenomenon of warm weather, or at least good weather. They are generally committed by a car full of young men, who find a lone woman or child on a fairly deserted street. Sometimes the assault begins with the car pulling up to the curb where the

The maxim which says that "Rape is a young man's crime" does appear to be true, since the age range of the apprehended rapists in this study went from the mid-teens to the early thirties. But here again, the entire story may not be clear—perhaps old rapists don't get caught.

Chapter Six

Weapons of Rape

Even though they usually outweigh the victim and have taken her by surprise, many rapists carry a weapon. Many more tell the victim they have a weapon, but never exhibit it. Some carry no weapon with them, but obtain one in the victim's home before assaulting her.

One local rapist, who is attributed with about 300 rapes over a three year period, specialized in quietly breaking into a victim's apartment during the night and obtaining a large knife from her kitchen before awakening her. By the time the victim awoke, the man had the knife pressed against her throat. He also carefully wiped his fingerprints from it before he left, and never took the knife with him. Thus, if he were caught, which he never was, he would have no weapon on him.

Another rapist always obtained a pair of scissors from the victim's bathroom, then pressed it into her ribs as he made his demands on her.

Whether or not a rapist will use the weapon with which

he threatens his victim is a pressing question. Some victims have called the man's bluff, fought with him, and won without his having attempted to make the lethal use of it which he announced in the first place. Others have been badly hurt by taking this risk; some have been killed.

One plucky rape resister, after hitch-hiking her way into a panel truck driven by two men, found that they had plans to rape her. Despite the fact that the man who was not driving had a long hunting knife with which he threatened her, and despite the fact that they had positioned her in the back of the truck body, rather than on the front seat, she fought her way out, past the man with the knife, and past the driver. She lost a good leather jacket in the scuffle, but landed on the sidewalk otherwise unharmed, even though she leaped from the moving truck. However, her good fortune was not because the man was reluctant to use the knife. It was simply because she struggled with him so furiously, that he was never able to get into the proper position to do so. Also, she made her move before the truck got out of town so that there was little opportunity for the driver to stop and help in the process of subduing her. She was about five feet, three inches tall, and weighed not more than 110 pounds.

We found no cases where a gun was actually used to shoot the victim, although there are such cases on record in other cities, and probably are in Denver for other years. However, pistols were used to whip victims and beat them into submission on occasion. We also had a case of rape resistance, where the offender threatened two victims with a powerful hunting rifle and fired several shots near their feet to convince them that he meant business. However, he finally retreated peacefully when these two women used an unusual ruse on him.

There were many cases where the knife was used. Sometimes vicious wounds and lifetime scars were caused; in other cases, it was used as a prod to make the victim move according to the demands of the attacker. In these cases the victim received only small nicks over her body where the rapist had pressed the knife deeply to reinforce his commands, while raping her.

In some cases, a handy weapon, such as a tire iron, was picked up in the course of the attack, to use in beating the victim into submission, or to abuse her body with. In the attacks where no weapon was used, the victim was usually threatened with strangulation, and given a sample of this type of coercion.

Table 14

Weapons Used in Reported Assaults on Adults in 1973

(False reports excluded)

Weapon Used	Rape	% of Total No. of Rapes	Attempted Rape	% of Total No. of Attempts
Gun	63	21.0	26	15.8
Knife	92	30.7	43	26.2
Gun and knife	3	1.0	1	0.6
Gun and other	0	0	1	0.6
Knife and other	2	0.7	0	0
Other	17	5.7	8	4.9

50cc needle
screw driver
straight razor
club
scissors
coke bottle
tire iron
wooden stick
meat fork
ice pick
metal statue
shoe
arrow
coat hanger
hammer

	Rape	%	Attempted	%
TOTAL Cases Where Weapon Used	177	59.0	79	48.2
TOTAL Cases Where No Weapon Used	123	41.0	85	51.8

Table 14 shows the number and type of weapons used in the 545 rapes and attempted rapes reported to the police in Denver in 1973.

Obviously, there was a slightly higher percentage of rapes with weapons (59 percent) than attempted rapes with weapons (48.2 percent), which implies that it is easier to ward off the attacker if he has no weapon. This table confirms that the rapist's favorite weapon is a knife of some kind. While a knife seems to be the appropriate weapon for anyone committing rape because it can be used quietly, it would seem that this same reasoning ought to obtain in a burglary for any other purpose. Yet, guns seem to be more popular for other types of crime.

There is something peculiarly inherent in the act of rape which calls for the use of a quiet, maiming instrument. The prevalence of this especially chilling weapon may somenow be a testimonial to the violent and sadistic needs of the rapist. It may also have something to do with the financial status of the rapist since many are unsuccessful in other walks of life and may find it easier to obtain funds for a knife than for a gun.

Also, as pointed out previously, a knife may be obtained from the victim's own supplies. Whether or not this preference for the knife is peculiar to the Denver area is unknown. At one time, during the active career of the rapist mentioned above, who obtained his knife from the victim's own kitchen, a newspaper story was published on the activities of this rapist. His well-planned modus operandi was recounted in the story, and from then on, he had many imitators so that it became difficult for local law enforcement personnel to determine if a victim had been attacked by this particular notorious rapist or one of his emulators. Whether or not this affected the number of knives used in subsequent rapes is unknown.

We also questioned the victims and resisters whom we interviewed on the subject of the rapist's weapon. Table 15 shows the results of these questions, and the pattern is the same as that shown in the Denver Police reports for 1973. Resisters faced fewer weapons. And the most frequently used weapon was a knife.

Table 15
Weapons Used in Rapes and Attempted Rapes
(55 Interviewed Subjects)

Weapon	Rapes		Attempted Rapes	
	Number	% of Total	Number	% of Total
Gun	4	12.5	4	17.4
Knife	12	37.5	5	21.7
Gun and Knife	1	3.1		
Other	2	6.2		
Knife and Other	1	3.1	—	—
Total cases where weapon was used	20	62.4	9	39.1
Total cases where no weapon was used	12	37.5	14	60.9
TOTAL CASES	32	100.0	23	100.0

Chapter Seven

Rape Resisters

Many women have successfully freed themselves from a man intent on rape, and they have used a wide variety of methods to do it. In most cases, these are not even reported to the police since if the woman got away unharmed, she merely thanks her lucky stars, breathes a sigh of relief, and goes on her way. It does not even occur to her to report it.

The common impression, among law enforcement personnel and practically everyone else who is professionally concerned with rape, is that women who resist a rapist are more likely to get physically hurt than women who simply submit to the rape. However, this impression arises from the fact that the rape resister who suffers a wound while fighting off her attacker is much more likely to report the incident than a woman who succeeds in fighting the man off without getting hurt.

This fact has become clear to me after giving many public lectures on rape and sexual assaults. After these talks, many women tell me privately about their experiences. I have always asked each person whether or not she reported the attempted rape to the police. Nine out of ten did not. Often there is little to report since the incident is over with quickly, the man is gone, and the woman has only a fleeting impression of his size and general appearance. There would be little point in notifying the police since she is not hurt and would probably not be able to identify her attacker. In other cases, she may know the man's identity, but since it would be his word against hers, and she was not raped or seriously hurt, she knows there would be no way to prove what happened, and again there is little point in notifying the police.

All this means that rape attempts are far more common than the published figures indicate. From my own work in this field, I now know that given any gathering of as few as ten women, regardless of age or social class, there will always be at least one woman in the group who has been raped or who has fought off a rapist. And this is a conservative estimate: in actual fact I have usually found as many as two or three even in a group that small. This means that at least 10 percent of all women have found themselves in this situation, many of whom have managed to prevent the ultimate degradation of rape.

It is true, however, that resistance may result in the woman's losing her life. In therapy sessions with fourteen rapists serving terms in prison, a colleague of mine tossed out this question to the group, "What would you do if a woman tried to resist after you had decided to rape her?" There was solemn and frank agreement, especially from the five rape-murderers present—they would kill her. Here again, however, our information is tainted by the way we have obtained it. These men had all committed sufficiently brutal rapes or rape-murders to have been committed to long prison terms; some were in for life. Rapists are not all the same, and these were obviously some of the most dangerous.

For that reason, some of the glib advice being presently

given out about what to do when faced by a rapist will result in some women being murdered. No one can give general advice ahead of time that will apply to all specific situations. The rapist who attacks any particular woman will be an individual with his own degree of violence, sadism, and explosiveness. Therefore, each woman must do whatever she can in the given situation—and sometimes all that she can do will be to allow herself to be raped in the hope that that will save her life. Sometimes it does not even do that.

With that caution, I can move on to the methods used by the women who were able to resist an attacker bent on rape.

In general, we found that the woman was more likely to escape her assailant if the attack occurred outdoors rather than indoors. With an indoor attack, there is the problem of the assailant being trapped as well as the victim. If the woman screams loudly, but is unable to do anything else, the attacker may quickly exit the same way he came in—if that is possible. On the other hand, if it took him a half hour to break in quietly, and it might take him several minutes to get out again quietly, he may be somewhat trapped, and instead of leaving, might lunge for the woman to turn off her scream instead. This is especially true in an apartment building or other structure where a scream might bring in people who would interfere with his ability to get out fast, or at all. If it is obvious that the scream will not bring any help, then he will very likely force the woman to stop screaming, and go on with what he came in for. Therefore, the indoor situation is considerably more dangerous than the outdoor attack, primarily because there may be a perceived element of danger to the assailant himself which he may eliminate by violently silencing the woman rather than by attempting a hazardous escape.

One cannot always depend on the rapist working things out as rationally as this, but the victim attacked indoors should give some thought to what might happen after she screams. Sometimes, however, when the attacker's response is not completely logical, it is in the victim's favor.

The Facts of Rape

For example, one woman put up with a man who broke into her room for twenty or thirty minutes while he repeatedly warned her not to make any noise that would be audible to the other people in the house. The voices of the other occupants could be heard by the victim and the man who had broken in as he and she talked in whispers. He asked her who the other people were, how many men there were, and many personal questions about herself while she kept him at bay, and prolonged the conversation. When he finally reached for her body, her pent-up terror burst forth in a piercing and prolonged scream. After the long whispered conversation and stealthy movement in the room, the scream completely shattered the would-be attacker. He abandoned all caution and leaped for the window. But he had actually entered the house through the window in an adjacent, empty room. The window he now went for was cluttered with the victim's collection of potted plants. He knocked a couple over, hesitated, then turned around in desperation. The victim jumped off her bed, hastily swept the pots away and opened the window for him. He gladly accepted her help, leaped out, and was gone. This attacker had a gun, or at least claimed to have had one.

However, another woman accosted in her apartment in broad daylight flatly refused to do what the intruder told her to do, namely take off her clothes and lie down on the bed. Whereupon, the man went berserk, wounding her so severely that she hung between life and death in a hospital for the next forty-eight hours. But the reason he left and did not finish killing her was that her baby in the next room started to cry. He could easily have killed the baby too, in the same manner as he was frantically attempting to kill the woman. Instead, as the sound of the baby's crying became insistent, his mood switched abruptly again, and he left. This was a case where there was no one to hear an outcry, either from the woman herself or from the baby. This may have been a factor in his berserk bludgeoning of the woman, but why the ordinary sound of a baby's crying caused him to stop will probably never be known.

We found, in many cases, that timing of the victim's resistance was highly important to its success. Some women, but very few, went along with the rapist part way, and then looked for and found a chance to escape. But this procedure is dangerous. If the man has successfully exerted control over his victim part way to his objective, then he is likely to become violent if she tries to turn the tables and attack him or get away from him. Most successful resistance occurred immediately. It had the effect of catching the attacker off guard and thus giving the victim escape time. Sometimes, it apparently had the effect of convincing him quickly that he had met his match and should retreat. From these cases we inferred that the least dangerous resistance was the early one. The resistance was often a matter of verbal response and attitude rather than physical force. We call this "psyching" out the attacker because it involves taking control of the situation out of his hands, and dominating him before any physical coercion occurs. Here is an example of it:

A public health nurse left her office late, and was walking toward her car, when a man suddenly appeared beside her, blocked her way, and said, "Move, bitch, into the alley! I'm going to screw you!" She stopped short, turned, and looked directly into his face. In a calm almost kind voice, she said, "If this is the only way you can get a woman, there must be something wrong with you. Why don't you come on down to our Mental Health Center in the morning, and we'll help you."

The would-be rapist stood perfectly still for a few seconds. Then he averted his eyes from her steady gaze. "Where is it?" he mumbled, his head down, and his feet shuffling.

The nurse took his arm, and turned him half-around. "Right over there in that corner building," she said. "Come to the front desk at 8 o'clock and ask for Dr. _____."

The nurse went home unharmed, and the Mental Health Center had a new patient the following morning.

The rapist seems to rely on shock and terror to bring his victim into immediate submission. He comes upon her suddenly, announces his intention usually in the most degrading terms he has available, and often issues a few epithets to her such as, "You whore," "You cunt," or the like to further reduce her self-confidence. This is often effective: the woman shrinks in horror and pleads with her attacker not to harm her. When he gets this response, the attacker has the upper hand from then on. He may or may not have a weapon, but the fact is that a man bent on possessing and perhaps violating a woman's body, appearing suddenly at her side in the dark, either on the street or in her home, is

Table 16

Methods of Resistance Used by Victims of Attempted Rape
(False Reports Excluded)

Methods of Resistance Used	Number of Victims
1. Screamed and/or cried	33
2. Screamed and took action:	
a. Screamed and fought	33
b. Screamed and ran	2
c. Screamed, fought, and ran	6
d. Screamed and talked	7
3. Fought	15
4. Fought and took other action:	
a. Fought and talked	2
b. Fought and ran	18
5. Ran	14
6. Talked	16
7. Act interrupted	13
8. Unknown	6
TOTAL	165

(According to Denver Police Department Sex Offense Reports for 1973)

enough to strike terror in the heart of any woman. Whatever she does after that point takes courage. Those women who manage to stifle their terror and turn upon the man in quickly assembled rage, or who can assume the cool but negative stance of the public health nurse mentioned above, can often take the play out of the rapist's hands and start issuing the commands themselves. It will not always work, but it is always worth a try.

Table 16 shows the methods of resistance used by victims of attempted rapes in Denver in 1973 who reported these attacks to the police. Screaming, with and without other action, was the method most often used by these women. In most of these cases, there was at least slight injury and/or tearing of clothes, or loss of the woman's purse. Most injuries were in the form of bruises from being knocked down or beaten.

Note that sixteen of the women represented in Table 16 merely "talked" their way out of the situation. These are some of the cases of "psyching out" the attacker by turning the tables on him as in the case of the public health nurse. But not all rapists allow the victim time to talk. Some refuse to engage in any conversation at all and also force the victim to be silent.

Tables in Chapter 4 show the types of situations in which rape victims (Table 9) and successful rape resisters (Table 10) were attacked. It is apparent that the situations in which the attacks occurred were much the same for the two groups, but that success in resisting an attack is somewhat dependent on situation. In other words, only 35.3 percent of rape victims (Table 9) were attacked outdoors, as compared with 43 percent of the successful resisters (Table 10). Apparently, it is somewhat easier to escape from the outdoor attack. But both tables indicate that the indoor attack is more frequent: 59.3 percent of all rapes (Table 9) and 52.1 percent of all attempted rapes (Table 10) occurred indoors.

The mean age of victims was almost exactly that of

resisters when all women age sixteen or over were considered as a group: the mean age of rape victims was 24.3, the mean age of rape resisters was 24.1.

Table 17

Mean Age of Adult Rape Victims and Resisters

Ethnic Background	Rape Victim		Rape Resister		t test
	No.	Mean age	No.	Mean age	Significant
Anglo	228	24.2	124	23.8	no
Black	32	25.8	11	23.1	yes (.02)
Chicano	35	24.6	21	26.1	no
Other	2	19.0	2	23.5	*
Unknown	8	18.8	9	23.3	*
TOTALS	305	24.3	167	24.1	

*Numbers too small to test for significance of difference.
(Data from Denver Police Department Sex Offense Reports for 1973)

However, when victims and resisters are broken down into ethnic groups as in Table 17, an age difference shows up: the black resisters were significantly younger than the black victims. This leads to an interesting point.

We looked at the ages of victims and resisters because we thought that perhaps the women who had successfully disposed of the rapist by whatever means, might possibly represent an older group; that possibly their increased years and consequent increased social presence had made them better able to cope with a threatening situation. However, this was not the case, as is shown in Table 17. Instead, for blacks at least, the resisters turned out to be significantly younger than the victims when a statistical test of the difference between mean ages was performed.

The ages of these victims and resisters only go down to sixteen years. We did not set up a category for rape resistance under sixteen since in the cases which were not completed rapes, it was often unclear from the child's story whether rape might have resulted or whether the offender's objective was simply molestation or sexual abuse rather than rape. Therefore, we have no group of "resisters" labeled as such under age sixteen.

However, it became apparent that in many cases, the response of the young girl, from age eleven on up through the early teens tended to be a more instant, physical reaction than that of a fully mature woman in her twenties or older. We infer that during those early teen years, physical activities, including fistfights, not only with other girls but occasionally with boys, are much more a part of her world than they will be after she becomes an adult. Therefore, an early teenager is much more likely to respond quickly and with her fists, than a woman ten years older.

One case that occurred during the course of this study was particularly illustrative: a thirteen-year-old girl was abducted and taken to a motel room where her abductor proceeded to rape her. He had forced her to submit by means of a knife which he had threatened to use on her. When, in the course of the rape, he put the knife down for a minute, she seized it and stabbed him with it. He then pulled it out of his body, even though he was badly wounded. As he lunged toward her with it, she caught the blade of the knife and broke it off before he could plunge it into her. The rapist died of his wounds.

It seems likely that one is more willing to take such high risks at an earlier age. In any event, if the "under 16" cases which we put into the category of sexual assault were to be sorted out, we would probably find quite a large number of rape attempts which were thwarted by the girls in their early teens.

Table 18 shows the comparison of the ages of victims and resisters whom we interviewed. These subjects are self-selected since they voluntarily answered our public appeal for interviews regarding the attacks made on them. Their ages (which represent age at the time of the attack) are similar to the mean age for victims and resisters who

Table 18
Mean Age of Victims and Resisters

Rape (N=32)		Attempted Rape (N=23)	
Mean Age of Victims	Standard Deviation	Mean Age of Resisters	Standard Deviation
26	8.0	24.5	10.1

*A t test for the difference between the mean age of victims and mean age of resisters was nonsignificant
(Data from Interviewed Subjects)

reported to the police during 1973. The mean age shown in Table 18 of twenty-six years for rape victims is not significantly different from the mean age of 24.5 years for rape resisters.

Section Two:

The Fictions of Rape

Chapter Eight

Myths and Folklore

To the Denver resident or visitor of a few years ago, Denver was a nice city. It always had been in recent years. Sprawled on the plains just east of the front range of the Rocky Mountains, it was not a city at all in the sense that Chicago, New York, or Philadelphia are. Rather, it was a collection of adjacent small towns. It still does not have the huge tenement areas of those cities, and since the day for building such monstrosities has passed, it probably never will. And Denver, unlike many large cities, has always had a well-deserved reputation for "friendliness."

But, while no one was looking, Denver grew up and acquired all the good and bad accoutrements of a big city. Fine old mansions serenely waiting out their years within a block or two of the downtown business district, gradually lost the settled, well-to-do families who built and occupied them. Other such families now build and live in the suburbs which were once the adjacent small towns. Some of the old houses were torn down and replaced by high-rise apartment and office buildings. Others were renovated and made into a number of small rental units. Still others were simply converted into rental units with little renovation.

Denver did not even have the appearance of a large city until recent years because it had few tall buildings. With the plains stretching away in all directions, there was no need for skyward construction. So Denver simply stretched out laterally, and most of the citizenry lived in one or two family houses and small eight- to ten-family apartment buildings. Thus, the dense population build-ups caused by block after block of many-storied apartment houses was unknown until recent years.

More and more as old homes were chopped up into dozens of rented rooms and small apartments, and high-rise living units cropped up everywhere, there were more and more people on the downtown streets at night. People who live in rented rooms and small apartments don't stay home much. And more and more small business along adjacent streets—drug stores, triple-X rated movies, magazine shops, short order restaurants, and pin-ball concessions—developed to help these people dispose of their evenings and their pocket change.

So crime came to Denver. Not with the gradual build-up that older cities experience as their populations increased, but in sudden leaps and bounds.

Attitudes, traditions, and municipal policy do not change that fast. Even now, with Denver standing near the top of all United States cities in the lists of various crimes, including rapes, you will hear old time residents and even some public officials say it isn't so. "Denver is a nice city," they say. And the only reason that it is shown at the top of such lists is that more crime is *reported* here than in other cities.

This would be wonderful if true, but it is actually just one of many ways of burying one's head in the sand. How can anyone determine whether or not more people are more prone to report crime in one city than in some other city? No one can accurately compute the number of unreported crimes in Denver or anywhere else because of the fact that they are unreported.

Denver is by no means alone in making this unsubstantiated claim of simply having more reported crime rather than more crime than other cities. This excuse is used by the residents and officials of many other cities as their fair metropolis surges upward in the crime statistics.

In an effort to get at the question of how much crime actually occurs and how much is not reported in each crime category, in various large cities, the U. S. Department of Justice conducted a survey from July through November 1972. The investigators contacted 9,700 households (21,000 persons age twelve and over) in each of eight large cities (Atlanta, Baltimore, Cleveland, Dallas, Denver, Newark, Portland, and St. Louis). They also contacted 2,000 commercial establishments. The interviewers asked, among other things, whether or not anyone in the household (or business establishment) had been a victim of a crime during the past twelve months, and if so, whether or not that crime had been reported to the police.

In every crime category, these interviewers found that many more crimes were committed than were reported. As always, rape was under-reported and in most cases in a ratio of 3 to 1. In other words, in most cities there were about three rapes committed for every one reported. Or, according to this study, only about one-third of the rapes that occur ever get reported.

Now, keep in mind that an employee of the U.S. government asked the question. From some people he received the answer that a crime had indeed been committed against them, which they did not report. This, at least gives a minimum number of unreported crimes. But keep in mind also, that if the crime was not reported to the police when it first occurred, certainly many people would not admit to this government investigator a year later that they had not reported it in the first place.

Many people living in large cities, as well as many in suburban and rural areas, particularly in this era of mistrust in government, tell the census taker, for example, just as little as possible.

To some it is clear that an interviewer for a given branch of the federal government has neither the interest nor the channels by which to report a rape that occurred a year ago to the local police. Nor would the local police have much interest in the matter if the interviewer did report it. However, a sizeable segment of the inner city population does not know this, does not believe it if it is told to them, and is not interested in trying to comprehend the bureaucratic lines of authority which make this so.

A general distrust of all "government" officials—census taker, police officer, and senator alike—seals their lips. In many cases, the distrust which deterred them from reporting the crime in the first place, will keep them from admitting to the Justice Department or other government interviewer that they failed to report it—especially when their answers are to be taken down by this "government" interviewer and entered on an official "government" form.

Therefore, the question of how many unreported crimes are committed is one for which only minimum answers can be obtained. In other words, if 500 rapes are reported in a given year, and the government survey obtains information from the individuals questioned that another 1,000 were committed but were not reported, then all we know is that *at least* 1,500 rapes were committed that year. Many women who failed to report in the first place will continue to keep the information to themselves when the interviewer comes to the door.

Therefore, since it is clear that no one—census taker, politician, or policeman—has an accurate count of the number of crimes committed, how can anyone truthfully say that more of the committed crimes are reported in one city than in another? All we know for certain is that the reported rates are higher in some cities than in others.

There is considerably more evidence that the reason for a high rape rate lies in the attitude "It can't happen here" than there is evidence for a higher rate of reporting.

Whenever the crime rate rises—any crime, any city— the immediate recipients of public ire are the police. The usually dormant public sentiment is aroused in all quarters: good citizens speak out, newspapers challenge the local constabulary to do their job and protect us better, and angry notes accompany traffic fines, admonishing the police to go out and catch criminals instead of wasting their time checking the overdue parking meters.

But police cannot prevent crime, at least not in traditional lines of police work. In most instances, they can only enter the situation after a crime has occurred. They are, after all, law *enforcement* personnel, not guardian angels. They cannot arrest citizens for looking as though they might commit a crime, for harboring criminal thoughts, or for being quietly psychotic.

Therefore, wherever crime rises, as the rape rate has in recent years in one city after another, the police are forced into a defensive position by the citizenry, and repeatedly asked why the rate is higher here than in some other city.

The answer to such a question would be only a guess on the part of a highly qualified team of historians, sociologists, psychologists, statisticians, and computers. The poor police officer would be the last to know the correct answer. But it is he who is constantly faced with the question. Therefore, he, along with the city fathers on occasion, has to come up with something—and preferably something that will take the pressure off him. A "high reporting rate" is one such answer. But it takes only a minute of logical thought by someone not "on the spot" to see that such an answer is full of holes.

This is one of the most prevalent myths about rape, or about any other crime which suddenly rises, and its use is by no means restricted to Denver, Colorado. Nor is it used only by beleaguered police departments. City officials and local crime commissions, intent on maintaining a good image, will use complicated, pseudostatistics to show that in "our fair city"—wherever it may be—there is so much public trust, that every citizen takes his troubles to the friendly police department, whereas in City X, some miles away, there is little reporting of crime to the police even though a great deal more of it occurs.

At one time, I was uncovering information from rape victims which showed that not more than one-third of the actual rapes were being reported. At that same time, a minor city official was publicly announcing that "at this time, *all* rapes are being reported here." He did not use my data to arrive at this conclusion, even though it was available to him. Instead he used a scientific-sounding method of calculating how many rapes must be taking place, based on figures from previous years. The method used had no validity whatsoever, but the figures, when spoken fast before a group, seemed to come out all right.

This number-juggling on the rape rate is a product of recent years when rates have risen everywhere, and cities are hard put to find the reason, much less the solution. It is a fairly natural defensive technique. But the fact remains that any figures on the rape rate are minimum figures based on the number reported. And any figures on how many rapes are not reported can still only be minimal figures, except for those which are purely fictional.

There are other popular myths surrounding the crime of rape which have prevailed for many decades, even centuries. Despite the vast technological, medical, and psychological advances of our age, rape has been a hidden topic for so long, that many of these myths continue even though they have no factual basis.

Some of the more destructive myths follow.

"Nice girls don't get raped." The police records of any city can refute this one. But, of course, few people get to see the police records, and rape victims don't go around with a sign on their backs.

The fact is that the expression obviously originated some time ago, when the word "nice" had a circumscribed meaning. Nice girls did not go out unescorted; nice girls wore corsets; nice girls never let their ankles show in public; nice girls never laughed above a soft titter; nice girls, in general, were Dresden dolls on a shelf—or at least nice girls were supposed to give that appearance in public. In private, they may have had all the virtue and chastity of Madame Bovary, with perhaps somewhat better luck than she. But the Victorian version of womanhood maintained the illusion of "nice" girls, who were hardly human, but for whom there was a closely proscribed pattern of behavior.

The modern woman, who very likely earns her own living, and may partially or totally support her husband as well, could not move about in her busy world if she were to be weighed down with all these nineteenth century trappings, any more than she could play tennis wearing a bustle.

The expression comes from the era of the hoopskirt, when women were protected, waited upon, and supported by men. During such an era, a woman who was out alone at night was defying the mores of her day, and therefore she was not "nice."

While none of these mores exist today, the myth remains. Even more importantly, many people who would not actually use the outmoded expression, do maintain the attitude that the woman who gets raped is somehow morally corrupt. Just how that would be defined, in the light of present day values, is not clear since it still does not *exactly* label her a prostitute, but what is worse, something fairly close to it, while pretending to be as good as you and me. In general, it implies that she is out looking for sex. Since, at the same time, it is generally agreed, even in the "nice" women's magazines that sex is a natural, healthy pastime even for women, it is hard to see why she would be classified as not "nice" even if she were doing just that. But logic has nothing to do with the attitude expressed by this myth. The fact that the key word in it is undefinable in terms of the present day culture, makes it even harder to dispel since it is almost impossible, and always futile, to attempt to refute an argument based on an undefined concept.

More specifically, the following is a prototype of about 250 of the women who were raped during 1973 in the Denver area:

She is about twenty years old, and likely to be a virgin. She lives in a small, neat one-bedroom or buffet apartment near the downtown area, and she works as a secretary, telephone operator, nurse, paramedic, or other semiprofessional job nearby. She has moved here to take advantage of the job opportunities of a big city. Her home is in one of the smaller cities or towns within the state, or a nearby Western or Midwestern state. This is her first job after college or business school, or, she has taken time out from college to earn money with which to continue her education. This is the first time she has lived away from her parents' home, except during her college life. She is raped in her own bedroom after access is gained by a man who removed the screen, and forced her window open. As far as she could tell, she has never seen him before, and may have "seen" little of him during the rape since the entire episode took place in the dark. He held a weapon on her while he forced her to comply.

I met her again and again and again, each time with a different face. She was a very nice girl.

Confucius say: Woman with dress up can run faster than man with pants down. This pungent little homily is supposed to imply that the woman can always get out of the situation if she really wants to. What Confucius didn't know was anything about the details of how a rape occurs. The literal assumption is that it is done the polite way—by lifting the woman's dress. But this view is utterly naive. The fact is that rape is rarely a casual encounter. The rapist usually has the event well-planned in advance. The woman is taken by surprise and is always at a disadvantage because she is off guard. Our Denver studies showed that in 59 percent of the rapes and 48 percent of the attempted rapes, the assailant had used a knife, gun, or other weapon, with the knife being the rapist's favorite.

In about 15 percent of the cases, the woman was attacked by not one, but two or more men working together, sometimes as many as eight or ten—all of whom participated in the subduing and raping of one lone woman.

In other words, the woman rarely has a fighting chance, even if she were evenly matched with her attacker in physical strength and prowess, which she almost never is. The rapist figures this out ahead of time.

So, Confucius (and each of his modern followers) is not talking about a bona fide rapist; he is talking about some bumbling idiot who may never have had intercourse with a woman in his life and obviously is not likely to.

Most "rapes" are false accusations filed by women who are trying to "get even" with some man. Oddly enough, with no facts whatsoever to go on, this is a strongly held and prevalent viewpoint. When discussing rape with laymen and women who have had no previous direct contact with the subject, this is often their first comment. It always surprises me. Therefore, Chapter 9 is devoted exclusively to this topic, the reasons for it, and the facts concerning it since this matter needs detailed clarification.

"Rape is a black man's crime." This is not true. While in the past, there may have been more *convictions* of black men than white men for the crime of rape, particularly in this country, men of all races and nationalities commit rape on women of all races and nationalities.

"If women would stay home where they belong, they wouldn't get raped." Our study showed that half of the reported rapes for 1973 occurred in the woman's home. Many of these took place after the assailant, whom the victim had never seen before, broke into her home while she was sound asleep. Others occurred when a stranger either forced his way in through a door, or in some way convinced

the woman to let him enter by posing as a salesman, repair man, or investigator of some sort.

"The rapist is just a lonely guy who becomes infatuated with a particular woman to the point where he cannot resist his passionate urge to possess her." Since the recorded rapes for the full year cover an age range of victims from age three through seventy-four, and other sexual assaults were committed on victims from age two through eighty-six, it is clear that sexual attractiveness per se plays no part in many of these attacks. The rapist himself is generally fairly young—between the late teens and early thirties.

Therefore, simple "passion" as such is hard to imagine as his motive in raping a four- or five-year-old child, or a seventy-five-year-old woman. In addition, in many cases, the victim's location is obtained merely by checking the names of single women on the mailboxes of apartment building lobbies. Here again, he has never seen the woman before he attacks her; he merely knows that she lives alone and is quite vulnerable when she is asleep in the middle of the night.

Beyond these considerations, there is the fact that the attack rarely contains anything simulating "passion." Many attacks are brutal and cruel, and all are degrading, with violence standing out as the ruling motivation rather than any tender sentiment or endearing propositions.

"Rape is impossible unless a woman wants it." This widely held view acclaims a complete lack of knowledge of the facts of rape as it occurs. Defending lawyers have often played the oddly convincing game of illustrating the difficulty of inserting a lead pencil in the opening of a moving Coke bottle. It is difficult to believe that anyone could be convinced of the credibility of the above myth by such a puerile illustration of what it is not.

But lawyers often win cases by the use of simple-minded and untrue arguments which have great popular appeal. And juries, tired of the long days of evidence and complicated legal considerations are happy for the break provided by an audio-visual display, and a concrete, symbolic summary of the whole question—even if the symbolism totally distorts the picture.

A much more telling illustration would be to put a gun to the lawyer's head or a knife to his throat, and then inquire whether or not he now dares to disobey the order to drop his pants. This weapon and order should be supplied by someone twice the size of the lawyer. This would have a great deal more relevance to the rape situation than the Coke bottle and pencil routine, which assumes that the woman (crudely protrayed as the bottle) is perfectly free to make any movements she desires. Nor does it take into consideration the fact that the rapist does not depend upon sweet compliance for his sexual excitement. In fact, this is the opposite of the truth. Many rapists actually become sexually aroused by a victim's display of resistance. There is, after all, no pride of accomplishment in fighting a battle where the enemy is totally submissive. In other words, the "Coke bottle" is forced to remain in exactly the right position either by threat, by prodding with a knife, or by the rapist's fingers laced around her throat.

Chapter Nine

False Accusations of Rape

Public education is most sorely needed regarding the question of false reports of rape.

To anyone working in the field of rape prevention, it is a particularly infuriating experience—and it happens far too many times—when the topic of rape is brought up to have someone immediately say: "But most reports of rape are false anyway, aren't they?" This statement ranges from a question all the way to a positive declaration depending upon the occupation or status of the person making it. Sometimes it comes from professionals to whom charges of rape are a nuisance. Other people who make this statement are those who have as yet had little contact with this crime, such as middle-aged, nonworking women who are comfortably married and who rarely emerge from their suburban homes in the evenings without their husbands. One can, perhaps, forgive their ignorance.

Much harder to understand are the views of people who have taken only a quick glance at complicated statistics and who then glibly state a view which is only slightly less atrocious, and just as inaccurate.

Unfortunately, one of the first books to emerge on rape, erred badly on this point. John M. MacDonald's *Rape: Offenders and Their Victims* (1971) rendered an important service in bringing the problem of rape to public attention, but the book states:

> In Denver 25 percent of forcible rapes reported to the police over a period of one year were unfounded . . . a further 20 percent of the complaints of forcible rate were open to considerable question.

These comments, contained in the first paragraph of Chapter 11, "False Accusations of Rape," are grossly inaccurate.

MacDonald states in a number of places throughout the book that he is writing on the rape and attempted rape cases reported to the Denver Police Department during 1968. The Denver Police Department files show that there were thirty unfounded rape and attempted rape cases reported to them in 1968. This was 9 percent of the total of 334 rape and attempted rape cases, *not* 25 percent as stated by Mac-Donald. The breakdown, as shown in official police records, is as follows:

	Offenses	Unfounded
Rape by Force	220	22
Assault to Rape—Attempts	114	8
Total	334	30

How such a large error in computation could have been made is difficult to understand, but MacDonald does not state how he determined that thirty unfounded cases were 25 percent of 334 total offenses. Nor does he give any indication of how he came to the conclusion that "a further 20 percent of the complaints of forcible rape were open to considerable question." If there had been any such question about these additional cases, the police would have placed them in the unfounded category. But there is no indication in the records that police had any reason to doubt the validity of the remaining 304 complaints of rape and attempted rape—and the police are the first to question such validity.

The term "unfounded," when applied to statistics on crime, can mean many things. While some jurisdictions may reserve its use for those cases where the event reported (such as burglary, rape, robbery) did not actually happen, many others use it as a catch-all category for cases where no further action by the police is possible. In Denver (where MacDonald obtained his data on this subject) the police have used the category "unfounded" as such a catch-all.

I found 131 victims whose cases were unfounded out of the total of 1,150 victims of all sex offenses (including rape, attempted rape, sexual molestation, and obscene phone calls).

For rape and attempted rape alone, there were 545 victims reporting; seventy-one of these victims subsequently had their cases assigned to the unfounded category by the police. A reading of each of the unfounded cases brought to light a long list of reasons for unfounding cases, only a few of which had to do with an actual false report. (This list is reproduced at the end of this chapter.)

For example, nine cases out of the total of 131 victims were unfounded because these cases were originally reported to the Denver police, but were found on further investigation to have actually occurred outside of their geographical jurisdiction, and were therefore transferred to the appropriate police department in a neighboring jurisdiction. This in no way implies that a rape had not occurred or that a false report had occurred. It simply meant that in these nine cases, the victims, some of whom were left stranded after the rape, called the wrong police department.

In many of the other unfounded cases, the victim simply failed to keep her appointment with the police detective, and the case was dropped. This still does not mean that no rape occurred, or that the original report of it was false. In many cases, a victim is threatened and harassed by the rapist and his friends into dropping the case. Also, it is well known that many rape victims who were living alone at the time of the rape, return home to their parents in another state, or move in with a relative or friend in another town as soon as possible after the rape because of their fear of going back and living alone in the apartment where they were attacked. They also obtain unlisted phones. For these reasons, it may be impossible for authorities to locate them, and the case is dropped. Many victims fail to go through with the police investigation because of shame or horror.

Also note that there are many other reasons for cases being unfounded which do not even imply, much less prove, that there was a false report of rape.

In order to separate out these incidental reasons for unfounding cases from the actual false reports, we read every case and designated it as a "false report" only if (1) the victim finally admitted that she had originally lied about being attacked, or (2) the police concluded from other evidence that she had lied. When these criteria were used—which seem the *only* appropriate reasons for calling a case a false report, we found thirty-five such cases. This constitutes 3 percent of the victims whose reports of a sexual offense committed upon them were determined to be false reports. (The exact basis for the determination of false report is shown at the end of Table 19.) Of these, fourteen were reports of rape or attempted rape to a woman age sixteen or over; sixteen were false reports of rape or sexual molestation *made by a child under sixteen years of age,* and the remaining five were false reports of various types of sexual offenses less severe than rape or attempted rape.

MacDonald's "25 percent" may have come from adding another category to the unfounded cases (although the text does not read that way): this is the disposition category labeled "exceptionally cleared." Here again, this category is used to indicate the disposition of cases where the police have done an investigation which leads them to a dead end. When the entire episode occurred in the dark or with the victim blindfolded, and she can give no meaningful description of her assailant, the case may be "exceptionally cleared"—but this does not mean that her report was false. In fact, in many such cases, the evidence is abundant that a rape did occur, but the police cannot conduct a search for a "medium-sized white male." If that is the only description they have, there is nothing to do but close the case. There are also other reasons for placing a case in the exceptionally cleared category. A complete definition of this category is shown at the end of this chapter.

The use of these vague categories and the inaccurate reporting of them in MacDonald's book have done much to confuse the issue of false reports, and to convince the public that false reporting of rape is much more common than it actually is. Even police are occasionally heard to express this view, despite the fact that their own departments publish data which refute their claim.

Since the rape rate has been rising everywhere, the publication of MacDonald's book with its incorrect statements that 25 percent of Denver's reports were false and another 20 percent were questionable provided an easy out for all cities with rapidly climbing rape rates. Since the incorrect figures indicated that nearly half of the cases reported (45 percent) were either definitely false or highly questionable, many people concluded there was hardly any problem at all except for the unfortunate tendency of women to lie. This is a classic case of slippery logic and sloppy research leading to a head-in-the-sand attitude which allowed everyone to relax comfortably while the rape rate continued to rise.

In addition, most of the reasons listed by MacDonald for women making false accusations of rape were taken from an article written by F. R. Bronson in 1918! Some important changes have occurred in our culture since then. Sexual mores which were in vogue at the end of the First

World War (1918) had already undergone vast changes by the beginning of the Second World War. The period of the 1960s saw further drastic changes, and now, in the 1970s, many of the concepts expressed in MacDonald, as well as the language he uses, are completely foreign to today's most rapable public.

The fact is, that in the latter part of the twentieth century, it is far too much trouble to report, identify, and prosecute a rapist for any but the very disturbed, or for the very young to try to do it when no rape occurred. The problems attendant on this process will be discussed in the next chapter. As a result, there are at least one hundred times as many cases of actual rape which are not reported each year as there are false reports of rape. (This figure can be checked by referring to the previously mentioned United States Department of Justice survey of unreported crime, and comparing the minimum nonreporting rate for rape—3 to 1—with the 3 percent false report rate discussed above.)

The typical false report these days is not the grieving Lady Windemere who regrets bestowing her favors on a lover who refuses to repay her with his family name, nor is it usually the stereotyped heroine of the 1940s whose indiscretions have placed her in a position which she dare not explain to family or friends. Rather, the typical false rape reporter of this era, we found, is an early teenager, who goes out with her boyfriend, or a small group of other young teenagers, and unexpectedly stays out all night. Sometimes the night's activities include sex, sometimes not. In either case, she returns home as daylight is breaking to find her home ablaze with light and her distraught parents pacing the floor. They may have already called the police and reported her missing. Faced with a hysterical and/or punitive session with her parents—and no good excuse—she may hastily concoct a story about a man, or men, who forced her into a car and raped her at some distant spot. The police are then called in if they were not summoned before, and she is taken to a hospital and questioned.

Alone with a detective, she finally breaks down and admits that it didn't really happen that way, but she knew that she would be severely punished if she had told her parents that she willingly disobeyed their curfew and stayed out that late with friends. She has not been raped, and this is a genuine false report.

For this reason, these days teenagers are often closely questioned, and their stories doubted by law enforcement personnel—sometimes unfairly, since in many cases an actual rape has occurred.

But, grown women in this half of the twentieth century, rarely give a false report of rape. In Dolley Madison's day it may have been the only recourse a woman had to "get even" with a man in retribution for real or assumed injustices. Today, women have many resources at their fingertips, including income, and they do not hesitate to use them. The reporting and prosecution of rape are altogether too complex, too cumbersome, and too unrewarding for any woman to pursue if no rape has occurred.

Also, since chastity is not the sacred cow it once was, accusing a man of defiling it may get less attention than accusing him of stealing one's stereo set.

Table 19

Reasons Behind Unfounded Sex Offense Reports

Offense Categories

A = Rape of a woman age 16 or older
B = Rape of a girl under age 16
C = Attempted rape, age 16 or older
D = Child molestation other than rape
E = Sexual assault, other than rape, to an adult woman
F = Sexual assault on a male victim of any age
* indicates that case has been considered a false report on Table I

No. of Victims	Reason for Unfounding	Offense Category	No. of Cases
9	Offense occurred outside city limits, therefore no crime committed in Denver	A B C E	4 3 1 1
*1	Discrepancies in victim's story	C	1
*1	Discrepancies in victim's story and unwillingness to go forward with case	C	1
*1	Discrepancies in victim's story and lab tests negative	B	1
*1	Discrepancies in victim's story and suspect didn't touch victim	E	1
*2	Two victims relating inconsistent stories	C	2
3	Victim lied about address and/or place of employment and detectives are unable to find her	A C	1 2
*4	Detectives believe offense did not occur as victim states	C D E	2 1 1
*1	Opinion of detectives that victim not telling complete truth since she refused to make identification or to testify	E	1
1	Victim unable to make identification; case refused by D.A.	E	1
1	Victim refused to cooperate with detectives by verifying offense, and lab tests negative	A	1
3	Victim refused to take polygraph tests and refused to go to court	A C	2 1
1	Suspect took polygraph and proved *he* was telling the truth	A	1
1	Victim took polygraph, which proved she had intercourse without force	A	1

No. of Victims	Reason for Unfounding	Offense Category	No. of Cases
2	Victim failed to respond to sex offense office for polygraph test and made report several days after incident	A	2
6	Victim failed to contact sex offense office, failed to keep appointment, or return detective's calls	A C E	2 3 1
1	Victim refused medical attention at city hospital and refused to take polygraph test	A	1
1	Victim refused to appear to verify report and make written statement	E	1
*2	Victim was drunk and can't remember what happened; lab tests negative	A	2
1	Victim belligerent and wanted to drop charges. Also, discrepancies in her report	A	1
1	Victim belligerent and detectives believe she is a prostitute	A	1
1	Victim moving out of state; no apparent motive for accused to commit assault. D.A. refused	E	1
5	D.A. refused case on grounds no crime committed	E F	2 3
*1	Conflicts in victim's statement and lack of "physical evidence." D.A. refused	D	1
*1	D.A. refused: insufficient evidence, and felt victim seeking revenge against suspect	A	1
1	Victim stated she wanted to forget whole thing. Told she must come in and sign no prosecution slip or case would be unfounded. Did not sign	A	1

No. of Victims	Reason for Unfounding	Offense Category	No. of Cases
*1	Victim decided it couldn't be called rape as she didn't resist advances to any degree. Signed no prosecution slip	A	1
*1	Husband stated he believed wife fabricated the story (rape). Police became aware of her paranoia	A	1
1	Victim's obvious mental problems as told by husband and past psychiatric history	A	1
1	Detectives could prove only intercourse, not rape	A	1
1	No force or threat sufficient for rape; D.A. refused	A	1
1	Victim not in fear for life. Didn't see knife	E	1
*1	Victim didn't wish to pursue case beyond report. Also, inconsistent stories, and past prostitution	A	1
*1	Victim not harmed. Gave wrong address and phone	E	1
1	Suspect didn't touch victim's private parts	E	1
1	Victim not sure if suspect lifted her dress or if it caught on his suitcase	E	1
1	No visible forced entry, and victim reluctant to be questioned about case (15 year old)	D	1
1	Victim reluctant to tell what happened. Officers observant of crime scene and lab tests negative (15 year old)	B	1

No. of Victims	Reason for Unfounding	Offense Category	No. of Cases
5	Any two out of these four: late report, failure to verify report, refusal to take polygraph, discrepancies in victim's story	C	3
1	D.A. states no crime committed (pinched on buttocks). Victim agrees	E	1
1	No obscene remarks, no threats, no series of phone calls	E	1
1	Victim refused to come to sex offense office and didn't want tap placed on her phone	E	1
1	No signs of injury to male victim. Mother does not want to press charges due to boy's problems	F	1
1	Suspect and victim married	A	1
1	No external actions precluding suspect from committing rape; attempted rape unfounded	E	1
9	Victim didn't see penis; indecent exposure unfounded	D E F	3 5 1
4	Suspect only touched victim's hand; no crime of assault	D E	3 1
1	Victim reluctant to have case investigated	C	1
*1	Victim has police record for drunk, theft, and occupying room with opposite sex. Lab test negative	A	1
*19	Victim admitted lying	A B C D E	4 3 1 10 1

No. of Victims	Reason for Unfounding	Offense Category	No. of Cases
2	D.A. refused since attorney had been engaged and case could better be handled in civil suit	D	1
9	Reasons unknown; incomplete report	A	4
		B	1
		C	2
		D	1
		E	1
1	Victim did not show up for polygraph, and discrepancies in interview	A	1
1	Victim did not wish to prosecute; police believe her to be a prostitute	A	1
*1	Victim failed to respond to detectives to verify report; victim paid for intercourse	E	1
1	Suspect entered apartment with victim's consent. Didn't touch victim. Insufficient evidence	E	1
2	Suspect didn't touch victim or use threatening or obscene language. Victim didn't see penis	E	2
1	Victim refused to cooperate; D.A. advises unfounded	E	1
*1	No creditable facts; victim's history of false complaints	E	1
1	No physical injury; assault unfounded	E	1
*1	Victim told too many different stories	A	1

(From Denver Police Department Offense Reports for 1973)

Section Three:

Problems Surrounding Rape

Chapter Ten

The Trouble with Being Raped

If you have been raped and are still alive, you will forever ask yourself *why* you didn't fight harder, why you didn't think of some trick to break away, or why you didn't engage in some other act—obvious to you now—which would have prevented the rape. Other people will also ask you.

If it happened on an August night and the rapist crawled in the window which you had left partly open to cool your bedroom, you will be asked why you didn't block the window in some way to prevent entry; why you didn't move to an air-conditioned apartment when the weather got warm; why you didn't realize that an open window, even on the second floor, is an irresistible invitation to a burglar or rapist. You will be forced to simply shake your head in shame and admit that you just didn't think about it.

If you were dragged under a bush and raped while taking a shortcut through a park, you will always regret trying to save those few minutes that the shortcut provided.

The ensuing rape used up not only the few minutes, but many hours of interrogation, testimony, nightmares, fear, and terror for several years to come. Other people will also question your judgment in taking the shortcut through a deserted area.

To some extent, it is always true when an accident or crime occurs, that it might have been prevented by adequate forethought on the part of the victim. You make a sudden left turn in traffic, figuring the distance a little too short, and get creamed by an oncoming truck. You forget to lock your car, and find that someone has stolen your camera out of the glove compartment. You leave your garage door open and find that a burglar has entered your house through the connecting door and has carted off the stereo equipment.

In all these cases, you chastise yourself for your carelessness. More finger-shaking is added by friends, neighbors, and perhaps the police, who will point out your lax security. But the chastisement—your own and others'— is limited to the carelessness which was directly responsible for the crime. No one will imply (unless perhaps you have received a large insurance settlement) that you were *trying* to be hit by the oncoming car, or that you *wanted* to lose your camera or your stereo equipment.

Not so with rape. The slightest evidence of avoidability will bring not only the useless questions: "Why didn't you . . . ?" but it will also bring forth smirks, innuendos, and sometimes outright accusations that you wanted to be raped.

To the victim, whose ego has already been beaten into the ground by the experience itself, this attitude is the last straw. Since rape rarely occurs with witnesses, she has nothing to rely on but her own insistence, especially if she was not visibly wounded, that she in no way wanted this horror that befell her. This is a difficult thing to prove and she knows it. Therefore, she must protest her innocence again and again, even if only to herself. All this either continues to destroy her ego or engenders an ever-increasing hatred and need for vengeance to the man who did this to her—or both. Since the rapist is rarely available to receive her ire, she may let it fly at some man who had nothing to do with the crime or against men in general. One can hardly blame her since the more guileless she is, the more she will resent the need to constantly reaffirm her innocence.

One way to avoid a great deal of this anguish is to avoid reporting the rape. Unfortunately, this also obliterates any chance that the rapist will ever be caught. Also, the fact that she does not report it, makes her look even more guilty to those in whom she may confide later on. But in the shock and horror immediately following the attack, many women cannot bear the thought of putting it in the public record by calling in the police.

While there are many individual reasons for not reporting rape, most reasons can be grouped under a few general headings. To make the victim's viewpoint clear, some specific situations follow.

Someone else will be hurt. This is probably the most common reason for not reporting rape as well as a number of other crimes. Despite the cynicism of our day, such altruism does exist, as the following case will illustrate.

Victim A was raped while engaged, with a number of other people, in what might be called a social experiment designed to extend help to a disadvantaged group of persons, most of whom were male. Being a sensitive person who was concerned with social injustice, Victim A decided not to report the crime since she knew that to do so would threaten the entire program of help to this neglected group. Whether or not the leader of the program should have allowed the helpers to be placed in a position of jeopardy with regard to the individuals being helped, may be questionable. Victim A knew that such questions would be raised. But she believed strongly in the leader and his goals.

So, even though the rape was brutal, she did not report it. Instead, she withdrew from public view for a week while her more obvious bruises healed.

Victim B, a twelve-year-old virgin, was raped when a friend of her high-school-age brother crawled in her open window in the middle of the night. Because of the location of her bedroom on the first floor, her family, sleeping on the second floor of the house, knew nothing of her ordeal until she presented herself to them in shock and horror after the rapist had left through that same window. But she knew who raped her. He lived in the same neighborhood; his parents belonged to the same church, shopped at the same stores as her parents.

The family talked all night in fury and in anguish. Morning came, with the father dashing off to his job still seething with rage. The brother cursed himself for ever bringing the friend to his home. Each family member took some part in the blame, and did his or her best to comfort the victim. No one thought about police, and since the victim showed no signs of physical injury, no one thought about medical attention to prevent pregnancy or to check for V.D. The female members of the family thought only of making the victim comfortable, and the male members plotted revenge. Help was sought many days later only because of the additional trouble caused by the revenge. But the rape was never officially reported since it would have devastated the family of the rapist.

I could not stand the shame of it. Victim C was seventy-nine years old when she was raped. She lived in a building with a security entrance, consisting of locked doors at the main entrance which could only be opened by residents, either using a key, or pressing a buzzer from inside their apartments. When a knock sounded at her apartment door, she readily opened it since she felt secure in the belief that only residents or their guests could gain access to the corridor outside her door.

But there are many ways to get through the "security"

doors of apartment houses. One way is to move on through with a resident who opens the door with his key. The resident will seldom object; instead he will assume the intruder lives there, otherwise why would he be fumbling in his pocket for a key?

The young man in his early twenties who stood outside Victim C's door that morning looked trim and neat. He belonged to the same age group as her grandsons who often dropped in to see her, sometimes merely passing through the security door as a resident opened it. The intruder asked Victim C if she knew which end of the apartment building contained Apartment 306A, as he had come to visit his grandparents, who had just moved in.

The number was unfamiliar to Victim C. As she paused, the intruder asked if he might phone his grandmother for directions since he had her phone number handy. Victim C cordially stepped back and invited him in—as she would have expected any one of her neighbors to do had her grandchildren been looking for her.

Once the door closed behind him, the clean-cut young man knocked Victim C against the wall with one backhand slap. He then grabbed her by the shoulders digging his fingernails into her flesh and demanded that she give him any money she had. Frozen with astonishment, she pointed to her purse on a nearby table. He dashed over, opened it, and tossed it down in disgust at the $3.58 he found. Pouncing on the terrified woman, he shook her, slapped her face, and hissed savagely that he would kill her if she did not produce some more. Shaking in terror, she made her way to the bedroom where she had always kept $40 in "emergency money" in case she were not able to get out to the bank. It would take care of the forgotten birthday of a grandchild, the taxi fare to her doctor's office in sudden illness, or any one of a variety of unheralded problems that might beset an older person. It would now take care of this unbelievable young man's demands, she felt sure. Opening the drawer in which she had it hidden, she first came to the small collec-

99

tion of quarters she kept for the laundry facilities down the hall. With a sudden inspiration, she handed him that. Seething with contempt, he knocked the small jar of change out of her hand, scattering the coins across the room.

Quickly she reached again, and came up with the $40. He grabbed it exultantly, and gave out a nasty whoop of triumph. "Thought you'd trick me, didn't you, Grandma!" he chortled. "Why you stupid old bitch. . . ."

With that he took hold of her again, and as she tried to pull away, his grasp ripped her dress at the shoulder. Terror streamed from every crease in her face. Hideous laughter issued from her attacker as he tore the rest of her garment away with one vicious wrench of his hand, threw her on the bed, and leeringly raped her.

When he had gone, she came to as though she had awakened from a bad dream. In fact, for a while she thought it was just that—a bad dream—until she saw the remnants of her clothing on the floor, and realized that except for her corset, which was up around her waist, and except for her torn and twisted stockings, she was lying there practically naked. Although she had never gone to bed half naked in her life, she still could not believe it until she inched herself to her feet and crawled over to the drawer where her special fund had lain for so long. It was gone. And there were quarters strewn across the room.

It had happened, she told herself. It really had. But another part of her mind could not accept it. She had been widowed for years, and sex was something that departed with her husband. Young men in their twenties were grandchildren—kind, solicitous, and gentle with her. They brought her presents, inquired about her health, and took her out to dinner on her birthday. She could not accept the reality of what had happened, even though her head throbbed from the vicious slaps, and her whole body ached and writhed from what could only have been a nauseating nightmare. She moved heavily into her sparkling pink bathroom, and became very, very sick.

Hours later, she strained up from the cold tile floor, and knew she had to do something about something. She was cold and sick and thought about calling her daughter at work. But what could she tell her? That a terrible, terrible thing had either happened to her, or that she had dreamed it, but either way she needed someone to help her, to talk to her, to cry to—but what then? Her daughter would come running, she knew, but what good would it do? Dream or reality, no one could change it, and once her daughter knew, she would tell the rest of the family. They would all come. But how could she ever face any of them again over the dinner table after admitting that this terrible thing had happened? Her physical discomfort led her to more immediate action which held no conflicts. She turned on the hot water, finished disrobing, and painfully crawled into the bathtub to remove all sense of what had happened, and relax her aching limbs. Then, emerging soaked and scrubbed and feeling at least physically cleaner, she firmly decided to put all thought of it behind her and she resolutely continued her chores for the day.

But from then on, the sound of her buzzer, or the tap of a well-known neighbor's knock on her door, froze all her senses. She stood rigid until the knocking stopped, and her neighbor went away puzzled at her lack of response. Days went by when she sat very still and never emerged from her apartment. Nights were spent at her kitchen table dozing because she could not bear to lie down on that bed again. Finally, when her son came and found her shriveled and looking as though twenty years had passed since his last visit ten days earlier, he took her to her doctor himself. It was only then that she haltingly admitted what had happened. She never told the police.

I was afraid he would come back and kill me, or my baby. Women living alone, with one or more small children are frequent targets of the rapist. Some of these women are divorced, some widowed, some have husbands who are away in the service. In many cases, the woman works, and either has a relative or friend come in and mind the children while she is away, or, more often, she takes her child to a day care center.

Often the initial rape is a break-in, that is, the rapist gains entrance through a door or window with an easy-to-pick lock on it. In many cases, he has trailed the woman for several days ahead of time, unknown to her, and is aware that she lives alone—or at least that there is no man living with her. Once in the apartment, he discovers the small child and uses the threat of killing the child to force the woman to submit to him. One local rapist made a habit of holding a switchblade knife over a sleeping baby's abdomen and telling the terrorized mother that he would rip the child open if she did not do as he asked. No young mother was willing to call his bluff.

Most rapists give warnings to the victim after the rape, such as: "You're not going to call the police are you? Because if you are, I'll finish you off right now!" "If you tell anybody about this, I'll come back and get in just like I did tonight. But next time, I'll slit your throat." "If you go to the police, I'll come back and kill you because you don't know who I am or where I live, but I know everything about you."

With the break-in rapes, this is unfortunately true. The rapist knows the victim's address, and by going through her purse, which many of them do, he can easily find out her name, what kind of car she drives, its license number, and very likely where she works. All she knows about him is that he somehow found a way to break into her apartment, that he is medium height, has a low, medium, or high voice, and is either black or white. After he disappears into the night, she has no idea how close he may live to her or to where she works, or anything else about him.

Sometimes the rapist will tell the victim to call him Bob or Jerry and to recite various loving phrases to him while he rapes her. But when such a clue is given to police, and the actual rapist is found by some means, his name turns out to be Edward instead. Rapists are keenly aware that they are committing a crime, and they go to great lengths to keep their identity secret from the victim.

In the case of the victim with a small child, the threats turn on the victim's greatest source of vulnerability—her child. "I know where you take the kid during the day; if you tell the police about this, I'll kidnap him and kill him long before the cops get me." Or, "I'll come back another night and kill the kid before I screw you."

All such threats can be effective in keeping the victim quiet for a long time after the rape. Nor are they idle threats—in some cases where they were made and the victim reported the crime to the police in spite of the threat, the rapist has actually returned, apparently to carry out his threat—and walked right into the arms of the police.

That rapists do often return is well known. Some victims have been raped again and again by the same man—whom they do not otherwise know—before they have finally decided to ignore the threats and report it to the police. Others have simply put larger bolts on their doors, sat shivering inside the locked apartment, hardly daring to close their eyes after dark, and have heard the stealthy, but unsuccessful work on the lock of door or window, only to see the same man running away when they screamed.

If a rapist can set up enough fear in his victim so that she does not report the rape, and if he can manage to gain entrance to her home again and again, this simplifies his whole problem; anytime the need comes over him to force a woman into submission, he can return to this woman he has already subdued.

Since the rapist uses terror to force the woman to submit in the first place, it follows that his promise of returning and killing her or her child is effective intimidation. Also, since he forced his way in once, she is well aware that he might be able to do it again. This is often a strong deterrent to reporting the matter to police.

I didn't want my family (my husband) to know. Victim D, a young woman in her early twenties, completed her

103

training at a small college in her hometown, a Midwestern city with a population of about 20,000. Since there were no opportunities for her there, she obtained a promising job in her field, in the nearest big city, about 200 miles away. She found a small apartment in an older section of town, in a former mansion which had been converted into six dwelling units. It had a tiny kitchen, a bathroom, and a combination living-bedroom. For the time being it was cozy, the rent was low, and there were friendly neighbors her own age in the other small apartments. It was a convenient place to start to learn how to live away from home, and her work was located close enough so that she could walk there. Three weeks later she was raped. A man had come in through the unlocked back door of the old mansion, had easily forced the simple lock on her apartment door, and had waked her with the prodding of a knife at her throat.

To Victim D, life in the big city became suddenly harsh. She immediately gave up the cozy apartment, and moved in with a girl friend whom she had known some years before back home. She stayed out of work for several days pondering what to do and recovering from the attack. She wanted desperately to go home, but she liked her new job. She liked starting out on a career, and she knew there was none for her back home. She also knew that if her parents had any hint of what had happened, they would come immediately and insist that she go back. Wasn't this the kind of tragedy they had predicted?

She never told the police about the attack because word might somehow get back to her parents.

The extent of nonreporting of rapes is a difficult figure to come by. There are many estimates of this statistic now floating around which were arrived at by many different methods, most of which are not reliable. Probably the most convincing attempt was that made by the U.S. Department of Justice Survey which was described in an earlier chapter.

A survey recently conducted in the Denver area by handing out a questionnaire on attitudes about sex crimes included a final question which asked if the woman had ever been attacked with obvious intent to rape or if she had been actually raped. It then asked if she had reported the incident to the police. The form was filled out anonymously.

More than 200 women have filled out the form, and of those who admitted to such an attack, only about 35 percent state that they reported it to the police. This figure corresponds well with the Department of Justice survey for this area. Not more than one out of three rapes is being reported in this region.

Since the bulk of our research data consists of offense reports filed with the police, there is no way to approach this question through that route since all are reported cases. However, our interview data which were obtained from fifty-five volunteer rape victims and rape resisters does offer some clues although these should be validated on a much larger number of subjects.

Table 20 shows the number and percent of our interviewed subjects who were attacked by an assailant who was known to them. It also shows the proportion of these attacks which were reported to the police. The rape victims in this study reported 60 percent of these attacks by a known assailant to the police. But, the rape resisters reported only 25 percent of attempted rapes. When both groups are added together (rape victims and rape resisters) only 50 percent of the attacks by a known assailant were reported to the police.

Table 21 should be compared with Table 20. It deals with stranger-to-stranger rapes and attempted rapes, and again it is based on information obtained from our fifty-five interviewed subjects. It shows that 90.9 percent of stranger-to-stranger rapes, and 63.2 percent of stranger-to-stranger attempted rapes were reported.

Here again, we see a higher tendency to report when the rape actually occurred than when the victim was successful in warding off her attacker. In other words, rape victims are more likely to call in the police than are rape resisters.

But an equally interesting finding is that the stranger-to-stranger attack is more likely to be reported by both victim and resisters than is an attack by a known assailant.

Summarizing Tables 21 and 22, I find the more serious the attack, the more likely it is to be reported, and regardless of seriousness, both rape and attempted rape are more likely to be reported to the police if the assailant is a stranger.

Again, the small number of subjects represented in these two tables dictates caution in any generalization of the results, but if these relationships hold after many more subjects are added to the computations, it may indicate that the largest percentage of nonreported rapes are those which were committed by persons known to the victim. It also suggests that rape attempts which are successfully warded off by the intended victim are much more prevalent than any official records reveal since the successful resister is even less likely to report an attack than the rape victim. This has further implications regarding the possible number of active rapists in any given area.

If a rape is reported promptly, the police will always urge the victim to see a doctor immediately. In Denver, the practice is to recommend that the victim go to the city hospital, Denver General Hospital, and have the policeman escort her there. She is directed there because of the use of a special "Rape Kit," which directs the medical personnel in obtaining evidence, and in preserving it in a form which will allow it to be effectively presented in court many months later.

Once at Denver General Emergency Room, the victim may have to wait some time before being seen. In the first place, she must be assigned a special number by the computing system, so that she will not be billed for services since rape victims are treated free in the Emergency Room. No one can take care of her before she has a number, which is an unfortunate but realistic fact of our computerized lives.

Then she must wait until a member of the Obstetrics

Table 20

Assaults by Previously Known Assailants

Category	Total Victims	Victims Assaulted by Previously Known Assailant		Reported to Police		Not Reported to Police	
		No.	% of Category	No.	% of Category	No.	% of Category
Rape	32	10	31.2	6	60.0	4	40.0
Attempted Rape	23	4	17.4	1	25.0	3	75.0
TOTAL	55	14	25.4	7	50.0	7	50.0

Table 21

Stranger-to-Stranger Assaults

Category	Total No. of Victims	Victims Assaulted by Stranger		Stranger-to-Stranger Assault Reported		Not Reported	
		No.	% of Category	No.	% of Category	No.	% of Category
Rape	32	22	68.8	20	90.9	2	9.1
Attempted Rape	23	19	82.6	12	63.2	7	36.8
TOTAL	55	41	74.5	32	78.0	9	22.0

(Interviewed Subjects)

and Gynecology Department is free to see her. At Denver General, rape victims are seen only by doctors from this department. That practice is in the victim's best interests, but may sometimes leave her sitting and waiting in the emergency room for several hours. The resident is on duty in the Ob-Gyn Department where babies are being born. Unfortunately the prime hours for rape victims are the same as for the arrival of new babies. And, ironically enough, the victim who has just been raped may have to sit and wait for a baby to be born before she can be seen by the doctor.

In addition to these considerations there are some facts of human nature that may enter into the victim's discomfort. In the emergency room of any large city hospital, personnel become accustomed to the sight of blood, gore, and tragedy. Automobile accidents supply a great deal of the activity along with other life-threatening situations like gunshot wounds. No one can remain in a state of constant alert for eight solid hours every day or night of the week. Yet, everyone who comes into an emergency room is carrying some kind of emergency with him, some of which are more urgent than others. Emergency room personnel become inured to tragedy. They see too much of it.

When a rape victim walks in under her own power, looking only as bedraggled and upset as most of the other people there, and considerably less so than the bloody victims of automobile accidents, or the child with a fishbone caught in his throat, there is a tendency for the clerical personnel to regard her case as less urgent.

Also, since rape has traditionally been a subject either to keep under wraps or to joke about, there is a tendency for the clerical personnel, if it is a slow night, to pass around their own little jokes on the subject. This is rarely a joke about the victim who is awaiting examination, but that doesn't make it any less painful for her. Such remarks as "Sure wish somebody'd rape me one of these nights," or "Maybe that new doctor will catch me out in the parking lot," whispered and giggled by the clerical personnel to each other, are knives of cold steel to the rape victim sitting within earshot. To her, rape is not funny.

The examination itself may also have its disturbing aspects. Any rape victim is bound to be not only sore but jumpy. To again have that area of her anatomy poked at by a strange man is at the very least, not a pleasant prospect. Many doctors are aware of this and specialize in gentle treatment, particularly if their field is Ob-Gyn. At the same time, most are residents who are at the hospital in order to learn more about their chosen field. There is little to be learned in the treatment of a rape victim per se. It is mainly a matter of collecting and preserving the evidence. At some hospitals, the medical personnel resent what they have called "playing detective for the police department." They do not want to waste their time getting evidence, especially since it may mean that they will have to waste more time appearing in court on the case at a later date.

This attitude is largely determined by hospital policy; in a city hospital it is rare because cooperation between the hospital and the police is standard policy. But many private hospitals do not want to take in rape victims at all unless there is an accompanying medical problem, such as severe wounds, for this reason. They feel that they are merely performing services for the criminal justice system.

When a rape is reported, the victim automatically enters into the criminal justice system with all its complexities. Currently, in many states the system is being simplified for the rape victim, and many public and private agencies are being set up to care for her special needs. However, these improvements are recent, and in many areas they are not yet working smoothly. Hope is on the horizon, however, that the injustices and inconveniences of the past which awaited the rape victim on her trip through the system, will all be eliminated.

However, in the past these were many. Immediately after the crime is reported, the victim is urged to go to a hospital, preferably the city hospital for examination. After that, over the next few weeks, there will be detailed interviews with police detectives as they attempt to pin down the facts and if possible apprehend the offender.

Once the rapist is identified and in custody, the legal proceedings start. This means more interviews with the prosecuting attorney. By this time several months may have passed, and the victim would like to forget the whole thing. In fact, her first urge is to forget the whole thing, but that has been impossible due to the necessity to cooperate with police, hospital, and district attorney.

In the meantime, she is trying to put her life back together. If she lived alone at the time of the rape, she has probably moved in with someone else since rape victims are plagued by nightmares and anxiety attacks in the middle of the night. It is much easier to sleep if there is another person there. She has gone back to work, hoping that not everyone around her is aware of why she was out for several days after the initial attack, nor why she has to take frequent time off to confer with the police or district attorney about her case. She may have obtained psychological counseling, and has been told to get out and do things, have fun, try to put it behind her. This she is trying to do.

But, eight or nine months later, when she has only partially recovered her equilibrium, and her interest in a normal social life, she is told that her case will be coming up in court. The fear, the nervousness, the cold sweat in the middle of the night start to come back again. She knows she will have to face her attacker in court; that she will have to tell every detail of the story again in front of a jury, and any onlookers who care to attend the session. She knows her attacker's lawyer will try in every way possible to break down her story. And she knows that she should have had that broken lock on her window fixed long before—then there might not have been any rape.

She gets cold feet.

Going through the trial will do nothing for her. She is

already beginning to feel like herself again. It will only mean more time off from work, more pay lost, more rehashing of the most unpleasant event of her life.

She notifies the district attorney that she cannot go through with it. He urges her to do so, and after several upsetting phone calls, she finally hangs up on him and refuses to answer his calls. She becomes a No Prosecute.

In other cases, the victim simply moves away. She leaves town because the memory of what happened is too painful, and if she has no permanent connections in the town, no one with whom she may go to live, she returns either to her parents' home, or to that of a relative or friend elsewhere. These moves often take place within two or three days of the rape, and when the police attempt to contact the victim to have her come in and identify a suspect, she is already gone. Such victims also become No Prosecute.

The rapist himself is sometimes responsible for the victim's refusal to prosecute. Many times there is both direct and indirect intimidation. Such things as repeated middle-of-the-night phone calls, direct threats by relatives of the rapist, calls to the victim's family by the defendant's attorney all weaken her desire to participate in a trial that is not going to make her feel any better anyway. In one case, where a victim in a Midwestern city was going through with prosecution, the defendant's attorney called the girl's parents in an Eastern city at three in the morning to ask about the victim's previous dating habits. The victim had kept the fact that she had been raped secret from her parents since she felt it would needlessly upset them.

In this particular case, her fury at the lack of ethics of the defendant's attorney only increased her desire to prosecute. But in many cases, the tactic has resulted in the victim's dropping prosecution, which was exactly the intention.

In another case, two black teenagers, one age twelve and the other age thirteen, had been raped on separate occasions by the same man. Since the rapist in each case had kidnapped the victim in one police jurisdiction and raped her in another, the case was tossed from one district to another, and the victims were all but forgotten in the process.

Finally it came to the attention of a concerned woman police investigator in one of the jurisdictions. In trying to follow it up, she found nothing but resistance in the other police district and was told to drop it because black girls deserved whatever they got since they had no morals anyway. But the policewoman-investigator probed further and found that the accused rapist, who was also black, had a long list of rape charges which had been filed against him, all of which had been subsequently dropped. She also found that it was well known in his home area that he frequently bragged about the young girls he had raped, even naming names. She supported the two black teenagers in their desire to prosecute him and encouraged them to stick with it when their own resolve flickered.

Shortly before the case went to trial, with excellent evidence, the home of each of the teenagers was fire bombed. At this point, caught between fear of what he would do to them if they went ahead with the prosecution, and fear that he would be free to rape them again if they did not, they prosecuted. But many before them had been frightened into dropping the charges at this point, as these two would have done if it had not been for the help given them by the female police investigator. The rapist received a long prison term.

Table 22 shows the refusals to prosecute recorded in Denver for sex offenses which occurred in 1973. Note that of the original 1,045 sex offense cases for that year, only 332 were considered prosecutable. This means that of the other cases, some were unfounded for various reasons (see Chapter 9), in many the suspect was never apprehended, and for others the evidence was considered insufficient for successful prosecution.

However, of these 332 cases which could have been

Chapter Eleven

The Trouble with Police

Everybody has heard horror stories of the careless and even cruel treatment of rape victims by policemen. What has not been so well popularized are the personal stories of many rape victims who praise the consideration beyond the call of duty given to them by individual police officers. The fact is, that on any large city police force, there are bound to be some individuals whose behavior is less than perfect. Denver, Colorado, for example, has about 1,500 policemen, at least two-thirds of whom have never answered a rape call. Most hope they never will.

Police hate rapists more than any other type of criminal. There are cases on which police detectives have gone out on their own time and kept watch in an area where a rapist was known to have operated, in the hope of intercepting him in the act.

But one trouble is that the rapist is hard to catch. Often the victim's description of him is vague and general—she may have seen him only in the dark. Or, she may have never seen him at all since some rapists blindfold their victim before she has a chance to get a look at them. This gives the police little to go on even though the rapist may strike again and again. And, unlike a robbery or burglary suspect, there is no way to find evidence of the crime, such as stolen goods, once the rape has occurred.

Most large cities now have a special group of trained detectives to handle the sex detail. These men and women are generally aware of the special characteristics of the rape situation, and it is fairly rare for a charge of police insensitivity to be leveled at the members of such groups by a rape victim. More often, victims are agreeably surprised at the extent of their kindness and consideration.

But these are not always the ones who first attend the victim after she reports the crime. The first man there may be a patrolman with no experience in taking rape calls or in handling an hysterical victim. He is there because his was the patrol car nearest to the address given by the victim, and speed in answering a rape call is important—the rapist may still be lurking somewhere in the vicinity. It is at this point in the encounter with the police that the insensitivity usually occurs.

If the woman has bathed, changed her clothes, and combed her hair in order to make herself presentable before the policeman arrives, he may scoff at her entire story. She doesn't *look* as though much has happened to her, and he hates to put another case on the record that will probably never be solved.

Unfortunately, the emphasis of our culture on personal appearance, clothing, the use of the perfect deodorant and hair conditioner, builds in some automatic responses which are sometimes inappropriate. The woman who has been raped and worked over for an hour or so cannot bear the thought of answering her door and admitting a neatly dressed policeman who is a stranger to her without first cleaning the semen and blood off her body, getting rid of the ruined clothing that was ripped off her, and applying her favorite cologne to replace the horrid smell of the man who assaulted her. A warm shower lets her relax a bit before the policeman arrives so that she can control her hysteria. All this, besides making her story unconvincing, loses the case for her since she has destroyed the best evidence—the blood and semen on and in her body, as well as the torn clothing.

The response of immediately cleaning up is a natural one, but the rape victim should avoid it despite her physical and mental discomfort at remaining the way the rapist left her. Because we are hounded with advertisements for products designed to eliminate, cover up, or disguise the fact that we are live organisms, this is hard to do. The fact that Jacqueline Kennedy, on the day of her husband's assassination, remained all day in a blood-spattered dress was cause for considerable comment, wonder, and astonishment. The usual response would have been to immediately go into consultation with fashion experts, and emerge hours later to express shock and grief in just the right Oleg Cassini gown, in an appropriate color, with matching accessories. The fact that she employed a different value system and took no time out for this was such a departure from our mores and expectations, that it was remarked about in every newspaper in the country. That she allowed her picture to be taken in the blood-spattered dress was shocking. Because of the times and the emotional context of the event, her actions even caused deep admiration. But when viewed objectively, what else would have been appropriate? Since her husband had just been murdered in front of her, and he also happened to be President of the United States, weren't there more important things for her to do than change her dress? And wouldn't any one in that situation be caught up in larger emotions than looking her best for the cameramen?

But we are so well trained by the advertisers in the need for beauty creams, fingernail hardeners, and properly curled eyelashes that her response seemed astonishing and bizarre. To a culture with a different value system, *any other* response would have been incomprehensible.

This is the automatic reaction of the rape victim that proves to be her undoing. Since men have traditionally been somewhat less burdened with the barrage of propaganda on appearance than women, the policeman is baffled at the sight of a clean, freshly dressed woman who claims she has been forcibly raped. He also knows that whatever evidence might have been there before he came, is now gone, and he is probably wasting his time making out a report. Even if he succeeds in finding the rapist, the case will be lost in court.

But the above is not the only reason that policemen sometimes exhibit no sympathy. Policemen are protection oriented. They are well trained to be alert to threatening, suspicious, or unusual situations. They are armed at all times, and they travel in pairs for protection. Since their uniform makes them just as much a target as womanhood, they take precautions against being caught off guard or walking into a vulnerable situation. Even in their private lives, these precautions never stop, the vigilance is rarely neglected—which is why newspapers often carry stories of captures and arrests being made by "off-duty policemen." Policemen who are caught off guard, who neglect to be vigilant and cautious wind up dead. An error may be lethal, and all other policemen go over the details of police killings with painstaking care to determine whether or not the death might have been avoidable with proper care and/or forethought.

To gain insight into the strict rules of precautionary behavior which police impose upon themselves within their own circles, one should read Joseph Wambaugh's documentary *The Onion Field*. In that suspenseful recounting of the murder of a Los Angeles policeman, Wambaugh carries the reader through the agonizing recriminations of the dead policeman's partner, who barely escaped with his own life. Even though the situation in which the two officers found themselves seems unavoidable to the average citizen, the policeman who escaped with his life was officially and unofficially condemned by his fellow officers for not preventing the tragedy or at least handling it differently. Controversies still rage within police circles about whether the two policemen did or did not take the right action. Since one died, and the other was ruined, the harsh conclusion generally is that they did not. Yet, the reader of Wambaugh's impartial account finds himself wondering what else either of the officers could have done under the circumstances.

Given this background and training, when a policeman answers a call from a torn and beaten young woman who states that she was just cruelly raped at 2:30 A.M. in an alley leading off of a deserted street in a crime-ridden area of town, he is likely to first demand to know what she was doing there alone, unarmed, and unprotected in the middle of the night. The response that she was returning from a party, a friend's house or a movie is unconvincing to him. He cannot comprehend the lack of protective instinct, or the naiveté, which would permit a 110-pound woman to walk alone at night through such an area. He cannot believe that she was unaware of the dangers of doing so since to him every dark doorway, every dimly lit bar, every passing car may conceal a potential attacker at that hour and in that part of town. Therefore, his only possible reaction is that the woman is either retarded, unbelievably stupid, or a prostitute. It is a long way from his training, background, and everyday habits to the unconcerned attitude of most women regarding the need to protect themselves by being alert to danger.

To the policeman, it is an obvious setup: no decent woman would be foolish enough to stroll to a movie or a party along a dark street at night where anyone she might meet has a better-than-average chance of being a drug addict, drunk, thief, or rapist. To the unfortunate woman, the policeman is a pig for suspecting her motives, and for not realizing that she has a perfect right to go anywhere alone. Little understanding can be transmitted between these two worlds.

For policewomen, the story is much the same. They have been trained to be observant and cautious. They also carry a gun. Few rapists would dare attack a policewoman in uniform. Yet some policewomen retain the memory of life before their training, and with it an enormous compassion for the victim who never had the advantages of such training. Julia Tucker of New York is such a policewoman. Her femininity transcends her uniform, and provides her with an understanding of the plight of the newly emancipated woman.

The fact that some policewomen have just as little compassion for the rape victim as some policemen indicates that the attitude is due more to the training than to the fact that the officer is a man. Yet that factor is there, too. For reasons cited earlier, most men (unless they have been in prison) have difficulty comprehending the horror of rape. Rape in prison does sound like a bad experience to them, but mainly because such rapes are committed by other men and do not provide a normal sexual experience to the heterosexual male. To be coerced by a member of the opposite sex into having intercourse perhaps sounds to most men like a free thrill, one which requires no excuses or elaborate fabrications. What an easy way to cheat on one's wife! It is hard for anyone to get into someone else's head and think the way he thinks. It is almost impossible to cross the line from one sex to the other and understand feelings that one cannot even imagine. Therefore, the average man, even many who have had training in the mental health fields, cannot empathize on any more than a verbal level with the fear and revulsion that a woman feels toward rape.

The policeman then has two strikes against him in his effort to sympathize with a rape victim—the first is that in the outdoor and easy-break-in rapes he cannot believe that the woman did not know in advance that this would happen to her since, given that same situation, he could easily have predicted ahead of time that it was highly probable. The second is, that if the woman shows no evidence of severe physical abuse he feels there is no real reason for her to be upset. Since she usually is upset when he first finds her, he feels that her attitude must be due to something else: perhaps the man didn't pay her; perhaps she wants to get even with him about something; perhaps she is worried that she will get pregnant and her husband will find out that she had sex with a stranger.

Police training and experience help. Certainly, if they can never really share the woman's repugnance, many come to believe in it, just as they believe in labor pains which they will also never experience. But what appears to be, sounds like, and sometimes is, sheer callousness on the part of police, actually stems from this inability to see the woman's viewpoint. One very fine and concerned policeman whom I met, in discussing the problem of rape with me, said, "I always tell women that the best thing to do if it happens, is to not struggle and fight, just relax and enjoy it as much as they can. That way they won't get hurt." This comment completely stopped me as I had thought, up to that point, that we were communicating. Then I knew that nothing had been transmitted but verbalizations, but I also realized that perhaps it was enough. His eagerness to do everything possible for rape victims was genuine even though it was finally obvious to me that he did not really understand their hurt.

And, recalling that so great and knowledgeable an authority as Confucius is reported to have made the same statement, I could hardly condemn the policeman.

That compassion, if not understanding, will quickly become more widespread is certain with the publicity now being given to rape. After all, the current consideration, care, and medical attention surrounding childbirth is a relatively recent development considering how long women have been suffering from it, and the sanitary napkin was not invented until the 1920s. In the meantime, many police departments are inserting a special set of lectures into their training programs for all police, not just those in the sex detail. This is a major step forward since it officially acknowledges the fact that sex crimes *are* different from other crimes in their effect on the victim.

Table 23 shows the number of 1973 sex offense reports which were cleared by the police either by an actual arrest or by the issuance of a warrant for the arrest of the alleged offender. False reports, telephone harassment, and obscene written material reports were eliminated from this analysis since there is little likelihood that the police can do much about any of these offenses unless they are connected with some other offense.

Clearance was obtained by the police on 27 percent of the remaining cases. The highest clearance category was Rape, Under 16, where 44.9 percent of such cases were cleared.

Table 24 shows the number and percent of cases in each sex offense category which were submitted by the police to either the district attorney or the city attorney. Starting with the 253 cleared cases which were submitted, only 152 were accepted for the filing of charges by either the district or city attorney. Thus, only 14.8 percent of the original 1,045 sex offense cases were finally accepted for filing.

Even after this point some cases will never go to court because the victim will drop the prosecution before the trial begins. Other cases will be plea bargained down to a lesser charge, and never go to trial for the sex offense. Still others will be tried and lost, the accused sex offender will be acquitted. Only a small percentage of the original total will result in convictions.

Since each of the original 1,045 cases required some investigation, and many of them required hundreds of hours of work, it is apparent that criminal justice is an expensive but not an effective process. It is also clear that

not all of the fault can be laid at the door of the police department. And it is obvious that the chance of a sex offender continuing to roam the streets even after the crime is reported is astonishingly large.

Chapter Twelve

The Trouble with

Women's Liberation

The rapist is, of course, easily recognizable as the ultimate male chauvinist pig. Not only does he regard his victim as a sex object, he regards her as a sex object who is forced to provide her services to him without his even having to contribute anything—not flattery, sweet words, support, or even courtesy.

Many rapists heap vilification on the helpless victim as they force themselves on her. In a recent gang rape, after abusing the victim for several hours, the gang members decided in her presence to "get rid of this piece of meat, and find another one."

Small wonder that women's groups have been interested in the increasing rape rate! At the same time, unless rape is accompanied by murder, it seldom rates more than a two-inch item on the back page of a city newspaper, and in most cities the name of the victim is omitted. Many rapes, unless they are accompanied by murder or a large robbery, are not newsworthy at all. What is there to say about them? "A 20-year-old woman was raped in an alley between X Street and Y Street last night. She was taken to City Hospital with multiple bruises and a possible concussion. Her assailant was a young man in his twenties. He was not apprehended."

Not much of a story, but to give the fine details would only be offensive to most readers. Besides, it happens all the time in big cities to unnamed "20-year-old women." Often she is from out of town anyway and not newsworthy herself. Nor does she want the news relayed to family and friends.

Therefore, many of the older and more solidly established women's groups, whose members are the wives of middle- and upper-income level executives, have been largely unaware of the extent of the crime of rape. Their homes are located in quiet suburbs which are rarely the working grounds of rapists. They seldom go out at night without their husbands, and when they do, they are likely to travel in a large station wagon with several other women rather than alone on foot.

The newer women's liberation groups draw from a different population. While settled, established, married, local women may be quite in sympathy with many of their views, and a few may join and become active in these groups, the large bulk of the membership is young, unmarried, and self-supporting. Many of these young women live alone and work in the inner city. In turn, these women are much more likely to travel alone, to walk from their downtown apartment to a nearby coffee shop, restaurant, or convenience store, to go to a movie alone, and, in so doing any one of these things, to get raped. They are also more likely to discuss the rape openly, publicly, and angrily with their friends.

For these reasons, and many more, members of the newer women's liberation groups have been vociferous in their outcry against rape. No one can fault them for this. At the same time, with local law enforcement personnel on the defensive and, for want of a better explanation, anxious to "prove" that the problem is not as bad as touted, and young "liberated" women full of new rights and anxious to use this crime to "prove" their case for male oppression, head-on clashes have been inevitable in city after city. Meanwhile the rapist goes on raping, and the victim goes on suffering.

Some of the issues are backed by logic; others are emotional and loaded with pseudofacts which start with phrases like, "Many studies prove that. . . . " (Such statements are always suspect unless followed up with a footnote which cites the title and authors of the studies, along with a complete reference which will enable the reader to dig them out of a library and read them for herself.)

I affirm the necessity for women's liberation. The fight for it is not new; it has been going on for generations, and many of us who have fought on this lonely battlefield since we were adolescents now welcome the new soldierettes to the fray.

Like all causes that suddenly become identified as a movement, women's liberation inevitably has some bizarre viewpoints and activities added to the rest. Perhaps it is even salutary since the public conscience is something like the old mule sold by the farmer: despite the farmer's caution to the new buyer to treat the mule kindly, when the animal failed to move on command the farmer socked him between the eyes with a board saying, "Of course, you've got to get his attention!" Bra-burning won no new rights for women— but it did get everybody's attention.

At the same time, new movements often sweep like a forest fire across the land, simply destroying everything in their path. Whether the women's liberation movement of the 1970s becomes a permanent, powerful force for elevating womanhood in all walks of life, or whether by its own hysteria, it reduces the female to a point of submission not seen since the Dark Ages, will depend on how rational the approach is from here on.

Public attention has been caught by the gimmicks, the

ruses, the slogans. Now it is time to prove that there was good reason to make the masses turn around and stare.

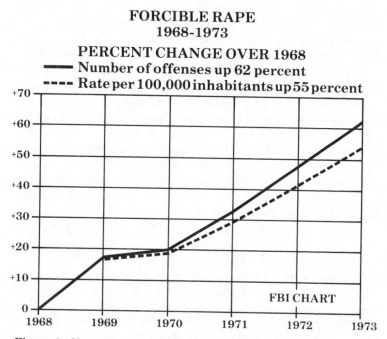

FORCIBLE RAPE
1968-1973

PERCENT CHANGE OVER 1968
—— **Number of offenses up 62 percent**
‐‐‐‐ **Rate per 100,000 inhabitants up 55 percent**

Figure 3. Changes in the Rape Rate from 1968 to 1973. From FBI Uniform Crime Reports, 1973, United States Government Printing Office, Washington, D.C.

The rape rate is rising everywhere. Figure 3 shows the increase over the years 1968 to 1973, as computed by the FBI in their 1973 Uniform Crime Reports. This is, and should be, of enormous concern to women's groups everywhere. But what are they doing about it?

Representing the police as inhuman pigs who do not care whether or not women get raped is not enough. Add to that, proposals for changes in the rape laws, and it is still not enough. Promulgating the idea that rapists should get longer and harsher sentences won't do the job either.

What is needed, and what can best be done by women's groups, is an enormous program of education for the women who would otherwise become tomorrow's rape victims. While there is much to be done in many areas, the easiest job of all—yet the one most neglected—is the job to be done in teaching the potential rape victim to protect herself. This is the part of "liberation" that has been sadly neglected by the "movement."

While on the one hand, through current literature women are imbued with independence, equality, and power, on the other hand, no credence is ever given to the very real fact that women are, and always will be, physically unequal to men and therefore physically vulnerable.

True, in a civilized society one's social and economic equality should not depend on the size of one's muscles or the effectiveness of one's left hook. But here's where reality must enter. What point is there in convincing a ninety-five-pound woman that she may exercise all her newly won rights without also explaining to her the responsibilities that go with these rights? If this is not done, she is in worse trouble than before she knew she had the rights.

Young women, before the age of puberty, are now being taught that they are exactly equal to men. Intellectually, this is certainly true and always has been. Physically, it is not true, and therefore, these women should also be taught to compensate in some way for the physical inequality that is a fact of nature.

In all jungles, including our highly mechanized one, the smaller organisms learn clever ways to keep out of the reach of the larger ones. Those who do not learn become victims. No sensible animal kingdom would survive where succulent calves were encouraged to wander freely among the lions, carrying only a flag with the words "calf power" on it. But this is the present stance of the young liberated woman! She will not survive.

Specifically, the problem is this: young women have eagerly bought their new freedom. They have readily accepted the doctrine that they are free to go anywhere without a male escort, that they have the same rights to hitchhike as men, that any job open to a man should be open to them, that they may use the same language as men. All of the above are reasonable propositions—if wisely applied.

But the fact is that even after being granted all the rights which she so richly deserves, a woman still has a woman's anatomy. No slogans or legislation will change that. Therefore, in putting to use her rights, she must at all times keep in mind that she is likely to be outweighed and outmuscled, and that this factor alone may determine her fate.

Emerging from centuries of being protected (and, admittedly the second-class status which accompanied it), most women are totally incapable of even thinking in terms of their own protection. This wariness must be acquired before the exercise of rights which place them in vulnerable positions. The fact that men do think in these terms is not so much a matter of "instinct" or hormones as it is a habit built up from eons of having to do so. There are many sections of every big city where no intelligent 105-pound-man (without prize-fighting ability or a track record) would stroll casually at 2 A.M. If necessary for him to do so, he keeps a sharp eye on dark doorways and alleys, clutches his billfold tightly in his pocket, and is ready to take flight at the approach of a group of locals. His flight will automatically carry him over fences, into a lighted area or anywhere else that the presence of other people will contribute to his safety. He doesn't have to think about it; most men, through a tradition of self-protection, react fast and effectively to personal danger situations. This is why so many rapists elude the police—and also why so many women do not elude the rapist!

If he cannot make a rapid exit from the situation, a man has a variety of fight and/or standoff techniques developed since he first entered a schoolyard, that may save him.

Women have no such history. They are not prepared either mentally or physically to even *avoid* such situations, much less to cope with them after they occur. It is not uncommon for a 105-pound-woman, these days, with no self-defense training whatsoever, to walk home alone through such an area of the city, without a thought about the loneliness of the street, the lurking shadows, or the car full of carousing men drawing alongside of her. When the men start to throw remarks and catcalls at her, she merely freezes up inside, walks a little faster, and tries to ignore them. She has no built-in reactions to this situation. Few women realize until they are told, that instantly turning and running in the direction opposite to that in which the car is traveling is the first defensive measure. It takes time for the car to turn around, and she can escape while the occupants are reacting. A long history of "decorous" behavior keeps her from shouting and making a spectacle of herself—but a loud and raucous scream while she runs in the opposite direction might save her from getting cruelly raped and/or killed.

These are the things which need to be taught to women before they are taught that they do not need a male escort in order to go out at night. The fact that the knowledge of the rights came first, without any training in the responsibilities of self-protection, has put many women in extremely vulnerable and dangerous situations. This is why the rape rate is rising.

Women are now in the same position as the developing nations where freedom has been newly acquired, in many cases before the knowledge of what to do with the freedom or how to handle the responsibilities of independence. The protection of the motherland is thrown off along with the exploitation that went with it, when the original purpose was only to get rid of the exploitation. This, then, makes the new nation vulnerable to exploitation by *all* larger nations. This is the position of today's woman unless and until she is thoroughly schooled in protecting herself while enjoying her new freedoms. The result of all this is the same as a new nation throwing off the relatively benign protectorship of Great Britain, and falling under the domination of Russia or Communist China, where even the second-class rights that obtained under the old relationship are denied under the new.

This is where the women's liberation movement falls short. This is where it unintentionally places its young converts in a more vulnerable position than they were a century ago when tradition, mores, and the inevitable protection of the men who "owned" them prevented their ever getting into many of the impossible positions they find themselves in today.

Unfortunately, many women who are now, because of their vulnerability, used and abused by men who take advantage of their disregard for self-protection, will retreat even further, sit cowering in their homes at night, restrict their activities, and pull their lives in close about them because of the fear that the horrible experience stamps into them. This, because the liberation movement has opened up the world to them with no preparation for meeting it competently. The backlash to all this may well be that women of the next generation will be overcautioned by these unlucky pioneers. The hard-won rights will be denounced as worthless because of the dangers that they bring with them.

This doesn't need to happen. The liberation movement should start now to train women for independence. It is, after all, a brand-new concept to the entire female population. And in this sense, women are the only newly emancipated group to whom that statement applies. Foreign nationals who find themselves in a minority in the United States or in some other country, did at some time enjoy full rights and privileges in their own country. There is a national, or ethnic, memory of freedom (however dim) and a national tradition of pride and independence. Women have no such group history. Therefore, the self-protective instincts of independence must be developed without precedent, and this must be done quickly within one short era—before the era disappears in fear that the whole idea was a mistake.

Despite the above, many women, both organized and unorganized, have done a great deal to bring the problem of rape and crime in general into public view. The efforts of Margaret Moore Post in organizing the women of Indianapolis against crime of all kinds, and on all levels, are certainly worthy of note. Marge Gates in Washington, D.C., has promoted effective programs locally and throughout the country; Julia Tucker and Mary Keefe of the New York Police were pioneers in focusing national attention on rape; Fran Mauck doggedly pursued a one-woman anti-rape campaign for years in Colorado Springs, and Jane Sternberg has done a similar job with only one staff member in Portland, Oregon. Kathy Saltzman organized rape prevention efforts in the Denver area; Susan Weeks coordinated these efforts. Geraldine Boozer in Florida has pioneered in the treatment of rapists, and the National Organization for Women has sponsored many effective lobbyists for women's rights in all spheres. Dozens of other individual women, whose names also belong in this list, from all over the country, have conducted dignified, rational campaigns to improve the lot of women in the seventies, and have concentrated on the problem of rape.

Unfortunately, however, many rank and file members of women's organizations and some such organizations themselves have adopted a program of tearing-down without the necessary corollary of rebuilding. For example, it is almost superfluous to note that it is a popular pastime of this era to denigrate police and law enforcement officials. Whether or not some individual police officers deserve criticism is certainly open to discussion. However, such criticism has its appropriate time, place, and form.

I have sat at meetings held for the purpose of inaugurating rape prevention programs with the cooperation of police officials. The officials present were not only cognizant of the problem of rape, but anxious to understand the victims' reactions to it and to work in conjunction with community agencies in educating the general public to take a more compassionate view toward this crime. Yet, sitting in these meetings were isolated representatives of the blatantly liberated woman, who casually referred to police in general as pigs, while sitting only a few feet away from genuinely compassionate policemen. Such phrases as "when the pig came to investigate," and "Yes, it probably would be helpful if the pigs conducted self-defense courses" flowed freely from these women while supposedly attempting to enlist the support and help of the police in preventing rape. The other women at such meetings not only felt embarrassment for this unbelievable display of rudeness, but were extremely concerned as to its effect on the success of the plans being formulated. In fact, it was sometimes necessary after these and similar incidents to make it clear to police, district attorneys, and other city officials who might be of assistance that we had no connection with either the group which these women represented nor with the women themselves.

Obviously, a few encounters such as this quickly turn local police off to all "women's groups," and the objective is never achieved due to the insensitivity of the approach. This is exactly what occurred in Denver, making the job doubly difficult since the more militant women took a firm stand against the police and never hesitated to express it no matter how unfair that expression might be in any given situation. Any woman who did not play this game was attacked as unfairly as were the police.

On the other hand, some police officers, unable to discern which women belonged to "women's groups" and which did not, quickly adopted a stance in opposition to women in general, privately considering them all hysterical (which many were in specific situations), while publicly giving lip service to the effort.

The attacks in both directions took many forms: on one occasion, a small local "liberated" newspaper published an entire issue on the subject of rape. This could have been concentrated on helpful advice on rape prevention to all potential victims in the area. Instead, much of the coverage was concerned with attacking the police, the city hospital, the district attorney's office, and in general citing how little was being done about the problem. Among other things, the newspaper printed the results of an interview with me—an interview which had never taken place—and even incorporated purely fictional quotes from me, which said that I felt that the police in this area were not doing as much as in other cities to combat the rape problem. It gave an example of what I supposedly thought the police should do, such as using decoys to catch rapists.

This was certainly no copywriter's slip since no reporter from the newspaper had ever interviewed me, nor had I ever made the quoted statements to anyone. But it was well known that I was one of the few direct links between women's organizations and the police. It was also known that I had openly disagreed with the practice of making idle, unwarranted public attacks on the police since I felt this accomplished nothing. Rather, in discussing this problem with various groups and individuals, I had stressed that the only constructive way to handle problems of police insensitivity was to publicly support positive efforts and to take specific criticisms directly to police officials in private so that the individual policeman who had erred could be reprimanded for his specific inappropriate act. This approach would not only encourage a spirit of cooperation between the community and the police, but would also assure individual officers that their commendable efforts would be appreciated and would not be smeared with the criticism due some other officer for his reprehensible behavior.

However, to the hysterical mind, anyone who refused to participate in or be a willing party to the generalized public attacks was viewed by the more militant women as a "pig lover." Therefore, manufacturing a quotation which attacked them publicly (even though meaninglessly) was a ploy to convey to the readership that a convert had been won over. It might also have the effect of destroying my working relationship with the local police.

Such maneuvers do nothing to help rape victims. Neither do they prevent rape nor solve any of the problems surrounding this complicated crime. Their effects are solely divisive, and the efforts expended by all concerned, first in perpetrating the controversies, then in straightening out the mess, are all subtracted from the time which could be spent on attacking the problems.

On another occasion, a rape trial was scheduled, and word was circulated that a contingent of women should attend the sessions. Basically, this was a constructive idea. Court-watcher programs, usually conducted by women volunteers, have been very effective in some areas in keeping both prosecution and defense attorneys within rational bounds, and in insuring that judges spend an appropriate amount of their tax-paid time in court. Too frequent recesses, too many late court openings, and too many early closings have quickly disappeared under the watchful eye of sincere court-watchers.

The rape trial opened with a large audience and with the impression that many women were there in order to become informed about the proceedings. However, a militant group quickly separated itself out and collected on one side of the courtroom. Interested police sat on the other side. It soon became apparent that one group of women was there for the purpose of intimidation.

The trial went badly for the prosecution. While there was little question that the witness had been raped, the defense presented overwhelming evidence to the effect that this was not the man who had done it. The defendant presented an airtight alibi with creditable witnesses confirming it.

When it became apparent that the accused might not be convicted, word went out from a self-styled leader of the unorganized group of women sitting in the courtroom to the effect that "If the law doesn't get him, we will!" Not only was this young woman (who had already been nicknamed Madame de Farge) vocal, but she was also reasonably well educated, which gave her pronouncements an aura of authority with the more impressionable members of her coterie. So the word spread.

My first notice of it was a frantic phone call from a sincere and hard-working young woman whose total effort was concentrated on the problem of rape prevention. Madame de Farge was known to both of us, and since she connected herself with the official rape prevention efforts in this area, having her promulgate this plan among the young women of the city, many of whom were rape victims themselves, could be dangerous.

It was necessary to take immediate action, and get word to her, through one of the grapevines, that those of us who took a more rational viewpoint, and who were truly interested in long-range rape prevention would become state's witnesses, and testify against her and anyone else who participated in a vigilante-type attack on the accused if he were found innocent.

The rape trial resulted in a hung jury. But police detectives expressed the view to me privately afterwards that the reason the accused was not convicted was because of "those rows of hostile women sitting there glaring at the jury and the defendant." Even court officers felt the jury was swayed toward sympathy for the accused because of the threatening belligerence of the block of militant women in the audience.

Many, many other instances of senseless antagonism and pointless infighting could be cited. None of them are of any help. Too much effort has been expended in this kind of activity.

On the other hand, a personal visit to a police station by one young woman who was involved in aid to rape victims, had salutary results. She discussed the problems of rape victims with the police captain and asked if it would be possible to have informed speakers meet with the men for ten or fifteen minutes at roll call, to interchange views on the topic of rape. The police captain not only consented but also set up a two-hour seminar to be conducted for the officers twice a week over the summer months, with speakers to be supplied by the young woman. From then on, members of the district attorney's office, hospital personnel, and other professionals who dealt with rape victims met with the police at that station. Much useful information was exchanged and many patrolmen on the line acquired a more sympathetic view of the rape victim, as well as a better understanding of her problems and of the functions of the organizations set up to help her.

Obviously, this accomplished a great deal more than the practice of publicly dismissing the police as "pigs," or threatening vigilante attacks on suspected rapists.

The antagonism, and with it the useless friction between groups both within and outside of the liberation movement, points up the fact that too much effort has been expended on changing other people's views toward women and not enough toward changing the views and behavior of the woman herself.

New words and phrases are coined by "liberated" groups. Then the use of the old term by a rank outsider is immediately condemned as "sexism," when, in fact, the user of the old term may actually be a devoted advocate of women's rights, but may resent being told which words may or may not be used. As with so many revolutions, the new leaders are just as dictatorial as the old! To legislate what words shall be used, and then enforce these not only on the membership, but on the rest of society, seems to be taking a page from the "establishment's" book. For example, the term "girl," by order of the women's liberation movement is no longer to be applied to any female who is over some ill-defined age apparently just before or just after puberty.

Instead, all recognizable females are to be called "women," and that only.

Any luckless male (or female) who happens to have his (or her) vocabulary well-established from years of usage, and who thoughtlessly refers to a group of his wife's friends as "you girls," will be viciously cursed by any "liberated" women in the group. This will also happen to any woman who uses the term "girl" to refer to adult females. And it will happen to man or woman regardless of how liberated their views and actions may be, simply on the basis of their not using the term specified by the rule-book of some "liberated" organization. Such uninformed citizens will be promptly labeled "sexist," with all the venom that might be displayed toward the vilest rapist.

The fact is that the term "girl" has been around a long time, and will probably continue to be. Its use can be loving, spiteful, tender, humorous, generous, flattering, disparaging, or demeaning depending on the intent of the user. Nor does the use of the term "woman" necessarily imply a benevolent attitude. It may (at this point) simply imply conformance to the code.

Instead of promulgating such useless issues, the fury now being generated at an outsider innocently using such a term could be much better channeled if it were appropriately directed. For example, women are traditionally nonviolent. This is a function of eons of being a "helpmate" rather than the chief aggressor. Women must be taught to strike out against *real* enemies. The man who thoughtlessly invites "all the girls" to lunch commits an indiscretion through not knowing what the organization has decreed about the use of that word and is totally unaware that he has erred. In other words, whatever demeaning effect the term may have is totally in the ears of the listeners.

But the rapist who forces a woman to submit to him is keenly aware that what he is doing is a crime and that it is degrading to his victim. Often he will go to great lengths to make it as humiliating and depersonalized as possible. Yet, many women have difficulty in effectively striking out at him, even when the strike would clearly give them the advantage. Many victims report that they "didn't want to hurt him," yet complain bitterly of how he hurt them, both physically and psychologically. The methods taught in many self-defense courses to enable the woman to jam her thumbs into the man's eyes and possibly poke them out make most women shudder. Many exclaim that they could never do that even if the man were killing them.

An episode in Diana E.H. Russell's *The Politics of Rape* recounts the story of a woman trapped by a man in his home, chasing her from one room to the next. He is unconcerned about any physical harm being done to her during the chase, and his announced intention (which he subsequently fulfills) is to rape her. At one point, she is in the laundry room, and quickly grabs a flatiron and threatens him. She holds him at bay with it. Later she admits that at that point she could easily have brought it down on his head and ended the chase. "But," she stated, "I thought and I thought about it, but, I don't know why, I just couldn't do it. So I put it down." The man then dragged her into another room and raped her in front of his young son.

It is not recorded whether he called her a girl or a woman, but certainly if the ire presently expended by women on the use of one or the other of these two terms were transferred into appropriate action in a situation such as this, it would do all women—and girls—far more good.

In summary, women's organizations should immediately divert some of the time and energy spent in unofficial hate campaigns to the problem of independence training for women. This effort should take many forms, from the use of money to the use of physical ability. Some of these areas are being explored by publications such as *MS* where articles have appeared on minor car repairs, and other topics designed to make women more self-reliant. Much more is needed, such as:

Self-defense for women—not long-range courses in the martial arts such as judo and tai kwando, but brief sessions in how to break away from an attacker.

Protection training—information on simple protective procedures such as walking against traffic, obtaining dead-bolt locks, remaining alert to potential dangers.

Newcomer advisory sessions—advice to young women newly arrived in a big city as to which streets to avoid late at night, high crime areas, where to obtain various services, and information on local helping agencies and crisis hot lines.

In the Denver study we found that 40 percent of the rapes reported in 1973 could have been prevented by the same simple precautions that one might take to avoid having one's purse or stereo set stolen.

Women's groups alone could therefore cut down the rape rate by that amount if they would inaugurate an all-out effort to train their members in the self-protection attitudes that must accompany the exercise of freedom. Otherwise, the liberated woman is a lamb being led to the slaughter.

Section Four:

Trouble-shooting Rape

Chapter Thirteen

Avoidance, Prevention, Escape

The crime of rape affects everyone. We women are all in the position of either having to guard against it or recover from its effects. All men are also affected for the same reasons. One of the most poignant reports I ever received was from a man whose wife had been raped. It was a particularly brutal attack, and in spite of his desperate efforts to help her through the ordeal and its aftermath, the results were tragic. It was he who sought help for her, for himself, and later for their marriage; and it was he who took care of their little daughter throughout the wife's mental breakdown and afterward. Their marriage never recovered.

Those men who have lost the primeval view that something that belonged to them has been despoiled (and there are many such in this era) are the most deeply hurt. If his chattel has been ruined, a man can always get another one. But there is no hurt greater than watching the suffering of someone you love; and the less chauvinistic a man is, the more he will suffer knowing how deeply his wife, daughter, girl friend, sister, or close acquaintance has been wounded.

Therefore, no one can afford to ignore the problem of rape, and no woman should fail to take precautions against it. This is something like stating that no one can afford to have an automobile accident because they are sometimes lethal, and no one can afford to have cancer. Both of these statements are true, yet there are those little slips which we all make, which result in a head-on collision, on days when our judgment is impaired by fatigue or concern about other matters and we take a shortcut which leads over an icy bridge. And there are other circumstances which just seem to fall on us from nowhere, regardless of how cautious we may have been.

At the same time, just as we invest in safety devices for our cars, keep our tires checked, and renew our windshield wipers; just as we make our regular checks for early detection of cancer, and hurry to have a suspicious lump removed before it is too late—in the same way, we should be vigilant about the possibility of rape. Some situations can be avoided entirely on certain occasions as having too high a probability to be worth the risk. Other situations can be prevented from happening by adequate forethought. Having done all those things and still finding ourselves suddenly faced with an attacker, women can use still other measures to get away without being raped. However, these latter, like radical surgery for cancer, carry with them a certain amount of risk.

In our Denver study, we found that 40 percent of the rapes during 1973 could have been prevented. In no case does this imply that the woman was attempting to seduce her attacker or that her clothing was too sexy or that what happened to her was due to "loose morals." The conclusion was based solely on such items as unlocked doors or windows, admitting a stranger to her apartment, picking up a hitchhiker, or accepting a ride with a car full of strange men.

This chapter will break down these situations into those which can be avoided, without drastically upsetting one's lifestyle, those in which a woman can effectively prevent the attack from ever taking place, and those unavoidable situations from which escape may still be possible.

Avoidance

In these situations, the woman takes some action to keep from placing herself in a vulnerable position. Many of the street rapes and those others which take place outside of the woman's home can be avoided. But only if the woman is always conscious of the fact that she is a target.

Walking alone at night: The gang rape. Gang rapes are on the increase throughout most of the world. They constitute some of the most brutal and certainly most traumatic of all rapes. They are often perpetrated on fairly young women; we have records of such rapes on girls as young as age eleven. The pattern of these rapes and their perpetrators are discussed in Chapter 5. To be completely safe from them, no woman, especially no young woman, should ever go out alone at night. With the younger girls, this is probably not a bad idea. But it is certainly not possible to either enforce, or submit to, such restrictions for many years after puberty. However, any young woman traveling on foot at night should be keenly aware that this is a real possibility, and its likelihood is not limited to ghetto-type neighborhoods or the downtown areas of cities. Given the right group of men in a car, it can happen in any neighborhood.

The simplest avoidance technique is to walk on the side of the street which will allow you to face oncoming traffic. This will not insure avoidance but if a car does come to a stop at the curb beside you, it is simplest from this position to start running in the same direction in which you were originally headed. The occupants may leap out, but it will take them a few seconds to disengage themselves from the car, which gives you a headstart. If anyone does start out of the car, a loud scream as you run, will usually send them back inside, and the car will speed on its way.

Under no circumstances should a woman engage in any conversation through the open window of a car with several strange men in it when she is accosted on a deserted street by the occupants, even to give directions. Men in a car can easily stop at a telephone or summon a policeman to help them find their way. No lone woman should feel any responsibility for aiding them unless it is an obvious distress situation. If she does give any directions, she should stay as far as possible from the car itself to avoid being dragged into it.

Rides should be arranged or a friend asked to accompany a young girl if she will have to walk any distance on a dark street. The friend doesn't have to be a large-muscled man. The main advantage is that two victims are harder to handle than one, and there is always the possibility that one will get away to summon help. There have been tragic instances of two young girls being picked up by a gang. If girls are in their middle to late teens, this is less likely. There are very few instances where a lone victim escapes without being raped, when there is more than one attacker.

Walking alone at night: The single attacker. Many of the same considerations apply as those just discussed for avoiding the gang rape, except that there are more possibilities for being overtaken by a lone attacker. At the same time, there is also a higher probability of being able to fight him off. Yet many women are raped by lone attackers, primarily because he catches his victim off guard, and secondarily because he is armed or says that he is armed.

To avoid him, watch out for dark alleys leading onto the street on which you are walking and stay as far as possible from them. Be alert to figures lurking in dark doorways. Look as though you know exactly where you're going, and go directly there without hesitation; in other words, don't look uncertain, wavering, or as if you don't know where you are or where you're headed. A firm step and a bearing of arrogance will brush off the less courageous attackers who are quite capable of demeaning you in every way possible, once it is clear that you fear them. In order to really carry this off, if you have to walk alone on the street at night, find out the exact directions for your destination ahead of time. Don't depend on asking strangers where the bus stop is, or how to get to such-and-such street. In short, the more independent you *really* are, the more you will convey that impression.

Be alert to footsteps coming up behind you. If you suspect they belong to a man, and you are on a relatively deserted street at night, turn and find out who it is before he reaches you. If he is contemplating attacking you, just the fact that you have seen him, and might be able to identify him later, may be enough to make him turn away, or at least hesitate. His hesitation should be used to your advantage— just as your hesitation will be used to his advantage. If you feel that his presence is at all menacing, walk directly across the street and continue to keep aware of his movements. If the other side of the street looks no safer, then stop in the middle of the street and face your potential attacker. You are always safer being attacked when you can see what the attacker is doing or is about to do. (Further comments on possible actions if the situation goes beyond this point are contained in the part on escape.)

Carry something in your hand which you might use as a weapon if attacked on the street at night. There are many small personal defense items on sale in drug stores and other places these days. Some of them contain either mace, or some other substance designed to temporarily disable the attacker by causing his eyes to burn so much that he can't see. These are legal in many cities if only used for self-defense. Check with the district attorney or attorney general in your area to be sure that these items have not been

151

outlawed. Some of these have the advantage of containing a red dye. When the red fluid is released some of it will fall on the attacker's face and clothing, thus making identification easier later on since the dye is difficult to remove. This will make prosecution much easier if the police are able to locate the suspect.

If you don't have one of these devices, carry something else which can be used as a weapon. Carrying a knife is dangerous unless you are well versed in using it and will do so when the occasion arises. For reasons stated elsewhere, many women are reluctant to actually use such a weapon. Also, it is too easy for an attacker who will probably outweigh you to take a knife away from you if you are at all hesitant about using it. He may be able to take it away from you anyway. A knife must be used at close range. If the attacker is that close to you, it would be necessary to be so proficient and definite about using the knife that he would be completely disabled at your first stab. This would take a fairly large knife and a determined thrust. Therefore, carrying a knife is not usually advisable. Carrying a gun is illegal in many places and may get you into more trouble than the attacker had in mind in the first place.

Keep in mind that if you kill or permanently injure someone in these situations, it had better be clear that he was about to commit a serious crime upon you. Your effort should be, rather, to temporarily stop him in order to give you time to get away or to summon help. Therefore, carry some item which will effectively do this, while not subjecting you to arrest yourself in case you panicked too soon and the man was only going to ask you the time. An eight or ten inch flashlight makes a good weapon. So does a heavy book, a purse with metal corners on it, or an umbrella.

Many publications on rape prevention currently being distributed, advise the use of a hat pin even though women have not worn such things for about fifty years, and most of us would not even recognize one if we saw it, nor know where to buy one. It is useless advice. A hat pin is about two or three inches long, and unless it is pushed firmly and directly into the heart or brain (through the eye) it is not likely to do anything but inflame the attacker. It has the same disadvantage as a knife in that it requires close contact with the attacker, and is far less effective than a knife after you do get that close. Its use in deterring a male attacker is evidently out of the cobwebby past where milady gently pricked a gentleman who too ardently "sought her favors," meaning that he reached out to touch her hand when she intended to be coy a bit longer. Its usefulness in warding off an attacker at night on a deserted city street is about the same as the ostrich feather which milady wore on her hat.

Picking up strangers. Many women have been raped, robbed, murdered, or all three, by giving a helpful lift to a strange man appearing to need a ride. Once the man is in your car, there is little you can do but follow his orders if he decides to take over. Usually in these circumstances, the man has planned the episode in advance and is carrying a weapon. With a gun or knife at your ribs, you are suddenly powerless to do anything but drive your car wherever he tells you to. Following a policy of never picking up a hitchhiker when you are driving alone may mean that you will leave many honest men to walk to their destination. But you will be safer.

Hitchhiking. This is by far one of the most dangerous activities a woman can undertake. There is no way to even estimate the number of rapes that occur each year due to hitchhiking because many are not reported. But among hitchhiking women it is well known that many of them have been raped. It is an inexpensive way to travel as far as money goes, but it's a form of Russian roulette.

The woman who stands by the roadside with her thumb up has no way of selecting the driver who stops for her. But whoever picks her up can easily have a plan. He alone knows what he intends to do, and cruising along a main highway looking for a female hitchhiker is far easier than climbing up the side of a building and breaking in by way of a second story window. It is also perfectly legal to pick up the hitchhiker: he has no worry that she will scream and summon help because she gets into his car willingly. He doesn't need to surprise her on a dark street, and take all the risks attendant on that course. Therefore, what better way for the sex offender to accomplish his purpose without coming into contact with the law?

If he finds out in talking to the woman that she is traveling through and is from a distant town, he need not even worry much about her reporting the rape since such victims seldom do. If she is a local woman, he can drop her wherever he pleases when he is through with her, and go on his way long before his description will be in police hands even if she does go to the trouble of reporting him. Besides, she was asking for it, wasn't she? She asked him for a ride, so didn't she expect to pay something for it?

The trouble with hitchhiking is that it is the first step toward placing oneself in a submissive position. The hitch-hiker asks for something free, thereby exhibiting dependence. The man also asks for something, the only difference being that he will not take no for an answer. Wherever one wishes to go, it is far cheaper, and considerably more independent, to get there under one's own power.

Prevention

In this section, the woman thinks frankly about the possibility of rape and takes steps to secure her situation to prevent its happening to her.

Drive with car doors locked. Most of us who drive a great deal have had the experience while waiting at a stop light of having one or more men step off the curb and grasp the door handle on the passenger's side. Usually, after their surprise at finding it locked and realizing that they can't leap right in, they bang on the window and ask to be let in. All you have to do then is shake your head, and move out when the light changes. If it isn't locked, you're in trouble.

This can happen day or night, in cities and in the suburbs.

Have your car keys ready when you approach your car. This is particularly important at night, or when you're in a vulnerable situation, that is, alone and there is a strange man standing around idly. Many women have been forced into their own cars in broad daylight in a shopping center parking lot, then commanded to drive to a lonely area where they were raped. If you approach your car, then stand there digging in your purse for keys, you are in no position to see anyone coming toward you from any direction. You have no alternatives if the man comes up behind you, presses a knife in your back, and commands you to get in and move over.

Choose your living quarters with security in mind. Avoid sliding glass doors, or secure them. These are too easy for an intruder to enter. Many break-ins for burglary or rape are made possible by sliding glass doors. If you do live in a house or apartment that has them, use a long bar or pole overnight, when you are alone, or when you're away, to block the track, so that the door cannot be opened.

Put fasteners on windows that cannot be locked. Even if they are on the second or third floor, unlocked windows provide easy entrance for an intruder. Burglar-proof fasteners for windows can be obtained at most hardware stores.

Install deadbolt locks on all outside doors, and if possible a simple burglar alarm that will sound off if the door is forced open after you have locked it. These too, may be obtained very inexpensively at your local hardware store.

Avoid dark entrances and long empty hallways. These provide a hiding place for an attacker.

Refuse to work alone in a deserted building. Overtime pay may come in handy, but a woman working alone in an empty, or almost empty, office building is in a vulnerable situation even in the daytime, such as on Sundays or holidays. Unless the building is small enough so that you can lock it and be sure that no one else can enter without your knowing it, the overtime pay will not be worth it.

Don't use deserted enclosed stairways. Many such stairways in older buildings have an outside entrance which will allow a man to slip in from the street and wait for ·a victim. In large newer buildings these stairways may be soundproof. Therefore if you are attacked here by someone lurking on one of the landings you can be forced down to the basement levels or into a storage closet without anyone in the building being able to hear your screams.

Take a self-defense course for women. Such a course will not only give you pointers as to your most effective means of breaking out of an attack, it will also give you the confidence to do so. Most women have never had any training or practice in physical combat. The average fourteen-year-old boy has more know-how in this regard than most adult women. A frequent response of women who are grabbed from the front by a man is to beat on his chest with her fists. This is totally useless, and is even pleasant and amusing to many men. A man's chest is one of the strongest parts of his body, and you will never break his hold on you that way. If you are taking the course purely for self-defense, then pass up the exotic sounding ones like judo, tai kwando, ju jitsu, kung fu, and all others which are classified as martial arts. These are all fine activities in which to engage for health reasons, and for the development of muscles you didn't know you had. But they *are* arts. They require a long time to master, and in this century are used mainly for tournament and exhibition purposes.

The self-defense course you take should be brief so that you can make full use of it within a month or two of enrolling. It should teach you which parts of a man's body are most vulnerable, and how you can quickly deliver a blow to them without endangering yourself. It should teach you how to escape from various types of holds that may be put on you and what to do in common emergencies of this type. These courses are often described as "dirty street fighting," which is exactly what you will have to know if you are attacked.

Escape

Escape is the toughest problem of all, which is why considerable emphasis should be placed on avoidance and prevention. Actually, each situation is different and must be handled according to the woman's own personal capabilities and self-confidence and her evaluation as to the violence potential of the attacker. All this must be computed in a few split seconds. Therefore, only suggestions, not concrete instructions, can be offered ahead of time for attack situations in general. With some attackers, and some situations, no escape is possible. Only later evaluation can determine which ones this applies to. Therefore, many ruses are worth a try; sometimes they will work.

The suggestions given here, for the above reasons, are merely accounts of what has worked for some people in the past. But, once attacked, each woman must judge for herself what risks she wants to take, and whether or not any of these escape ideas applies to the situation she finds herself in.

Try to take psychological control. Since the attacker relies on creating instant terror, catching the victim off guard, and rendering her totally subservient, anything you can do to reverse this may ruin his game. Many rapists are actually afraid of face-to-face encounters with women, and use the sudden attack as their only means of making contact. As I have mentioned previously, in most sex assaults, it is important to the assailant to keep the victim in the context of an object, not a person. If she can force herself on his consciousness as a thinking, reacting person, this also may help.

For example, the reaction of the public health nurse cited in Chapter 7 turned the tables on the attacker. The vile language of the approach and his stated intention failed to ruffle the nurse as the attacker intended it to do. She merely viewed him as a patient, and she advised him of where he might obtain the help he so obviously needed. It worked.

In another situation, a young woman was grabbed by a man as she was entering the back door of her apartment building. She had had a self-defense course, and instead of attempting to pull away from his tight grasp, with what little freedom of movement she had, she lunged at him, grabbing his shirt and ripping it. At the same time she verbally accosted him. He drew back in surprise. He had expected the opposite reaction. She followed up with further vituperation, and as his amazement caused him to relax his grip on her, she wrenched free to further pummel him in appropriate places as directed by her self-defense course. He took off running and went right over the back fence in his effort to get away from her. She was not over five feet, two inches tall, and weighed not more than 110 pounds. He outweighed her by something in the neighborhood of fifty pounds, but her reaction convinced him immediately that she would be too much trouble to bother raping.

A young girl of eleven was casually sauntering home from school one afternoon, when a grown man suddenly leaped out of the tall hedge beside her and pounced upon her. The man was middle-aged, heavy, and twice the size of the child. She fought, kicked, struggled, and bit until she was free of him, then ran. She could hear his footsteps coming after her. There was no one on the street in the quiet suburban neighborhood. Her own home was right on her way, but since her widowed mother worked, and her younger brother was still in school, she knew there would be no one home. She ran right past her own house, up the steps, and into the next-door-neighbor's house. The man then kept on running until he was out of the neighborhood.

Two young women were accosted in the woods by a man with a rifle. He informed them that he was going to rape first one, then the other of them, and that they could decide who went first. He convinced them, by shooting at their feet, that he meant business with the rifle. They tried to talk him out of it, but he was adamant. Finally, one of them decided on a "friendly" approach. She put her hand on the man's shoulder, explained that they would rather be friends with him and do what he asked, but it would be so much better as friends, not with a rifle pointed at them. The other woman took the cue, and she too petted the man's face with her hand and expressed her desire for him, but in a more romantic setting. The rifleman drew back in horror at their touching him. "You two are crazier than I am!" he hurled back, as he escaped from their caresses and took off.

A young woman was alone in the living room of her home in a suburban neighborhood one evening, when she heard someone entering the back door. She immediately went to the kitchen and found a man there. He had broken through the screen, reached in, and unlatched the door. "What do you want?" she asked. He stuttered at being caught so soon and countered, "I came to see if you want any trash picked up." This was obviously not true, and the young woman knew it. But, without faltering, she pretended to take him at his word. "I don't know, " she answered, "but I'll ask my father." With that she gave a loud call for "Dad!" The man bolted out the same door he had come in, and disappeared in the darkness. Her father was actually 500 miles away, and did not live in the house with her—but the intruder didn't know that.

One woman turned away a would-be rapist (who was later convicted of five other rapes) after he had gained entrance to her apartment simply by telling him in shocked tones that she could not go to bed with him since she was having her period. She pretended to subscribe to an old superstition which prohibits intercourse during that time, hoping that her attacker might be sensitive to the superstition. He was. He insisted on evidence, which fortunately she could supply. Then he apologized to her, *warned her never to admit a stranger to her apartment again,* and departed.

In another case, a woman dissuaded her attacker by

telling him that she had V.D. However, in still another case, a woman who actually was under treatment for syphillis told this to the man who broke into her home to rape her and warned him that he would catch it. But he scoffed at her story and raped her anyway.

In all of the above cases, with the possible exception of the eleven-year-old, the victim did something unexpected which put the assailant in a bad or uncertain position. In other words, she either one-upped him or intimidated him, and did it in such a way that he was still able to retreat. She took psychological control of the situation, even though in most cases she would have been unable to take physical control of it.

Many rapists are living with a psyche which does not permit them to make any of the normal approaches to women. They rely on the victim's response being, "Please don't hurt me. I'll do anything you say if you just don't hurt me." This allows them to move ahead with their original plan. Many also have *just one* plan. Note that in some of the cases cited in other chapters, the rapist uses the same approach again and again and again. If this plan is upset, he may be unable to shift quickly into a different one. Therefore, if the clever and self-confident victim-to-be can block one channel of his approach, or turn the encounter into something he had not planned on, it may be enough to make him retreat to try his usual approach on someone else, or to forget the whole thing for the time being.

These devices will not always work since assailants come in many forms. Most of the cases discussed above probably represent the shy introverted, loner rapist, whose appropriate social interactions with women were never established.

There are other types, such as the vicious brute to whom verbalizations of any type mean little. Some attackers order the woman not to talk and enforce this command with the prodding of a knife. This gives her little chance to move in on his personality with any ideas that might dissuade him.

There is no way for a woman to know which type she is facing, but most of the verbal ruses are worth a try.

The physical attack on the rapist himself is chancy if he has a weapon, but sometimes worth the risk if he does not. Unfortunately, it is impossible to say ahead of time, or to advise women in general whether or not this approach should be used. But this line of advice is currently being promulgated by a number of self-styled experts who urge women to "fight back"—to turn on their attackers with fists, feet, and claws, rather than to submit. (One proponent of this approach even instructs the women to "bite a piece out of his cheek, then save the piece for evidence!")

Advice to women to fight off their attackers is generally purveyed by six-foot-tall, 250-pound men. It may be quite appropriate for the average bar or street fight between males. But few women have the physical capacities, the self-confidence, the pugilistic skill, or the solid bulk to successfully follow it. Unless the victim's first few lunges are extremely effective in disabling her attacker, such a battle may only result in her being badly hurt—and then raped! A certain number of women will be killed trying to follow the advice to fight back.

The point of fighting back should be to inflict enough pain, confusion, or disablement on the attacker to enable the woman to get away fast. Getting closer to the man in order to bite, stick hat pins into him, or swing useless blows which neither disable him nor slow him down is pointless, and might only inflame him to the point where all of his physical power would be utilized to retaliate.

In a report of *The Crime of Rape in Denver* (see Giacinti and Tjaden in the bibliography), the investigators found that "if the victim does not fear injury, she can physically resist or flee the scene and in a great number of cases, will be successful in aborting the offense. Her chances of injury were however, found to be significantly greater." In other words, to fight, flee, or submit must be the woman's own decision at that split-second when the attack occurs. And the decision must be based upon the closed or open nature of the attack situation, her own abilities, state of shock, and self-confidence, as well as whether or not the attacker is armed, or *in the woman's judgment* is going to get violent.

Therefore, women should look with caution on specific advice about resisting an attacker. Most police officers do not indiscriminantly advise fighting back. This is because they have had the experience of picking up the remains of women who lost such battles. Men who do promote this approach are usually merely voicing what they feel *they* would do if threatened with bodily harm—which has little relevance to what a 110-pound woman can accomplish using the same tactics, or to the statistics which repeatedly show that untrained rape resisters frequently sustain bodily injuries. In some cases, these injuries may be preferable to being raped, but this decision can only be made by the victim.

In summary, if attacked, a woman should do the same type of thing that she would do if suddenly confronted by a shark while swimming—try to keep her head, take whatever action she is capable of executing, and, above all, do whatever she feels is necessary in order to save her life.

Chapter Fourteen

New Legislation Needed

The legal situation with regard to rape is out of step with society's needs. It has long ceased to be a naughty allegation that a shy vixen in hoopskirts whispered under her fan to a fatherly judge in order to avenge the cad who had accepted her favors then failed to ask for her hand in marriage. It is a much more earthy matter than that in the 1970s. It is a vicious street crime which will not abate until all social forces descend upon it. But even though women's groups may foster self-defense courses, even though self-protection awareness and independence become much more a part of women's behavior than they are now, even though the police become superbly diligent in hunting down sex offenders, it will all be for nothing if the end point—the criminal justice system—does not have the proper equipment with which to deal with the problem.

Several new approaches are necessary: (1) the victim must be placed in a better position from which to make her case, (2) the victim must not be expected to bear the burden of financial losses which she suffers as a result of being sexually assaulted, and (3) the legal system must provide, not for just the temporary restraining and punishment of the sex offender, but for appropriate treatment, in treatable cases, to insure that after his term is served, he will not be put out on the streets again to start the same process all over.

Some states now have begun to pass laws denying the defense attorney the right to bring up the victim's past sexual history if it is unrelated to the attack at hand. This has been a long time coming, and in the majority of states has not yet been enacted into law.

The problem here is that rape is still seen in many quarters as simply an overabundance of romantic passion, not as the crime of violence which a mountain of current data show it to be. Even a prostitute should not have to submit to being raped. The argument often put forth is that prostitutes will then use the law to get even with men who failed to pay them for their services. In the first place, few prostitutes ever bother to report a rape. They are generally wary of the police and the entire legal establishment, many of whom know them as members of their profession. Even fewer prostitutes, if they do report a rape, ever get beyond the first police interrogation session without being tabbed as such and their cases thrown out. Therefore, this argument focuses on a tiny minority of victims and punishes the vast majority.

To press the argument further, the fact that a woman has had numerous boyfriends, some of whom she maintained an intimate relationship with over a period of time, has nothing to do with the fact that a man knocked her down on the street, dragged her into an alley, and forced himself on her. This has no connection with a mutually agreed upon relationship that she may have had with a man of her choice who cared for her. This is the same as saying that because a woman spends her money randomly, anyone has a right to knock her down on the street and steal her purse. It is also the same as saying that because a merchant gave away a free television set last week, burglars have the right to come in tonight and take another one from him by force. The two activities are unrelated, but in the case of rape, the suggestion that a woman has had an active sex life *with men of her choice* is often used to prejudice an uninformed and unthinking jury.

The "Lord Hale" admonition to the jury, pronounced sententiously by the judge before the jury goes into deliberation, is now under attack (and is also being hotly defended) in some states. This admonition allows the judge to state to the jury that they should keep in mind that rape is an easy charge to make but a hard one to defend against. In present-day America, the judge is wrong. It is far from easy to go through the many interrogations, examinations, doubts, fears, innuendoes, and trials demanded by a charge of rape. In most jurisdictions, the case will never even get to court unless there is an avalanche of hard evidence against the suspect. District attorneys demand an overwhelming amount of proof before even presenting the charge and often refuse to prosecute cases turned over to them by the police (who have already refused to submit a large number of the cases to the district attorney), for lack of sufficient evidence. On the other end, as any lawyer knows, it is much easier to win the case for the rapist than to prosecute it for the victim. So, here again, we are dealing with antedeluvian concepts, imbued with the picture of milady coyly blushing behind her fan in the background while a fine gentleman in ruffled collar hangs his head in disgrace. In Lord Hale's day, it is doubtful that hospitals had already probed in milady's vagina for sperm before submitting the case to the magistrate.

In what other type of case is the judge allowed to make a prejudicial statement to the jury? Intent to commit fraud, "premeditated" murder, and conspiracy are easy to charge and difficult to prove, but are judges allowed to caution juries in one direction or the other on such cases? Why stack the cards against rape?

Many victims drop out and do not prosecute the case. This leaves many rapists free to rape again, even though the police may have spent a great deal of time and effort chasing them down and arresting them. If the victim will not prosecute, the charge must be dropped. Sometimes it is clear that the woman was actually victimized, sometimes it is not. But in many cases, details get forgotten, and it is assumed that the victim had no case. Why do victims do this?

Consider a victim, raped at knifepoint in her own bedroom in the middle of the night by a total stranger who came in the window. She called the police, told her story, and was escorted to the hospital to remain there most of the night, waiting and being examined. She arrives home a few hours after dawn, and calls her employer to say she will be out sick today. If she can pull herself together soon enough, there is an appointment at the police station waiting for her that afternoon where she will again tell her story. If not, she must go later in the week. She spends many hours away from work that week talking with police detectives. With luck, a few days later, the detective calls her at work to come down again and look at photographs of possible suspects. In the meantime, she has moved to another apartment to get away from the fear and nightmares she experiences all night long in the room where the rapist entered. She has now lost several days work, and her employer is becoming impatient with her. Yet, she does not care to confide in him the real reason for her absences. If the police pick up a suspect whom she has identified from the pictures, she will be asked to identify him again in a line up. More time lost.

Then the case is submitted to the district attorney. She must now be interviewed by this office, so that the prosecutor may see what kind of witness she will be and hear her tell the details of her story. The case is set to come up in court several months later. In the interim, the deputy who was to handle her case has gone on to other things, and she must be interviewed by another deputy. (She may go through three or four deputies before her case ever comes up.) She is also told, or otherwise finds out, that the case may be plea bargained. In other words, since she was not badly injured, the defense to be presented by the suspect's lawyer is that no rape occurred, that she actually consented to having sexual relations with him. Therefore, if she will agree to let him be prosecuted simply for breaking and entering—since the police did find evidence of this—the case can be quickly disposed of.

At this point, after all she has been through, the loss of work, sleep and self-confidence, and with the time she must spend in court, which is open to the public, still ahead of her, she wonders why she is bothering with this at all. She is not going to feel any better after it is all over. The rapist may only get six months in jail, and then be free to molest her again. She has already suffered a financial loss from the time spent away from her work, and she will spend more. She signs a no prosecution form, and decides to try to forget the whole thing.

Victims who do go through the entire process have to be possessed of considerable fortitude. The final degradation they must face is the sarcasm and humiliation of questions and comments from the defendant's lawyer. His purpose is only to save his client. What happened, or how, is irrelevant; many lawyers will do anything possible to ruin the reputation of the victim, in order to accomplish this. This will be her entire reward. So, why go through it—unless she is unswervingly devoted to attempting to protect other women from the man who raped her. And with the trauma of what actually happened to her still too fresh, still keeping her from enjoying a normal life, with her own life often in ruins, since she continues to jump nervously if a man comes too close to her even in a casual situation, let alone a romantic one, no one can blame her for turning the whole matter off by signing a no prosecution slip. Tomorrow night there will be another victim attacked by this same man, who is now free, to go through the entire expensive process again.

Lastly, there will always be a crowd of despondent rape victims, more every year, unless something is done about rapists. The traditional solution has been to sentence the man to a prison term of anything from a year to forty years, with the majority of sentences on the low end of this scale. He then enters an institution of caged men, many of them psychologically sick, as he may be himself, to sit out a life of terror until enough pages have been turned on the calendar. But even then, he is not like other prisoners. The social structure of the prison is such that various types of crimes command higher respect from the inmates than others. Murderers are at the top of the list and highly respected by the prisoner population. Rapists are at the bottom. He is the subject of ridicule, sadism, and homosexual rape himself during his prison stay. This is a man whose sexual responses were short-circuited in some way while he was a free man. Now, in addition to the restrictions imposed on him by the state as his punishment, he has a host of other restrictions, duties, and humiliating experiences imposed on him by his fellow inmates because he is at the bottom of their totem pole.

To many people, this may seem like exactly what he deserves in view of his own treatment of the victim he raped. Possibly so. But the longer view would ask what this accomplishes. If he had an uncontrollable urge to humiliate and degrade women before he went to prison, what will happen to this urge during the five or so years he spends suffering every possible degradation that idle minds are able to invent? How will he feel about women when he gets out? Will he now have kindly, normal views toward them and be prepared to accord them their rights, after a woman was responsible for his five years of hell? Unlikely. But he will probably not be caught raping one again. Prisons are highly advanced educational institutions specializing in sub rosa courses in how to evade the "fuzz." As a graduate of such an institution, with many hours of exchanging views with other prisoners on where each made his mistake and got caught for his particular crime, the rapist is likely to be a great deal more careful the next time. He will continue raping, but he is not as likely to get caught. So what has been accomplished?

Far better to place such persons in a situation where there is some possibility of treatment and retraining which will catch up the loose threads in their psyches so that they may engage in civilized behavior. The creation of social monsters who are then set free to prey upon the public simply because enough pages have been turned on a calendar is a custom which belongs to the Dark Ages. Modern society cannot afford to continue to do this. The criminal justice system is overtaxed, with prisons and detention centers overflowing, yet the practice goes on of putting men into cages, and simply turning them into animals, who will then be released on the innocent.

Some states are now setting up treatment centers instead. Obviously, it is necessary to restrain these offenders. But restraint without treatment of the problems which caused them to commit the crime in the first place, is merely postponing consideration of an adequate solution until another day. No one can restrain a man after he has served his time, and in many cases, the original problem has merely been compounded by the prison sentence. True, treatment programs, at this point, are not 100 percent effective. But releasing the man back into society is 0 percent effective since he returns with more trouble than he took in with him, and will now inflict his original vengeance plus his added humiliation back on society again.

Small wonder that crime is on the increase if this is our only solution.

Chapter Fifteen

The Treatment of Sex Offenders

Behind all the victim support systems, the self-defense courses, the counseling, the resistance techniques and the rape crisis lines is the man who is responsible for all this—the sex offender.

Most of the hundreds of new programs in this field that have sprung up in the last few years concentrate on help for the victim, increased street lighting, new legislation, and increased public awareness—all of which are necessary and appropriate. But these efforts are all after-the-fact. Attention must also be directed toward doing something about the direct cause of the problem—the man who commits the sex offenses.

In time, we must also probe the indirect cause, the society that creates this man. But the route to that investigation lies through the sex offender himself, and first we have to find out more about him.

Despite the rise in rape rates and the swelling public outcry against them, there is a surprisingly small amount of interest in sex offender treatment programs. The instant reaction to them by many people is that the best treatment is to lock up the offenders and throw away the key. But this is not possible.

Few sex offenders serve long penitentiary terms. Even rape-murderers have a good chance of walking the streets again. And the average rapist who did not murder his victim is certain to be released while he is a relatively young man. Therefore, something must be done to keep these individuals from committing more sex crimes when they are freed. Otherwise, all of the foregoing, and all other efforts at rape prevention are a matter of fighting the same brush fires over and over again.

But the next objection is: "Rehabilitation of sex offenders doesn't work, does it?"

At this point in the brief history of the mental health disciplines, what is not known about treating sex offenders would fill most of the cells they occupy. This is largely because treatment of them is new, underfinanced, and unpopular. Traditionally, sex offenders and been punished, not treated. And there is now enough experience with that approach to be certain that it does not work. Convicted rapists have rarely had the resources to avail themselves of years of expensive psychiatric treatment after their release. In the few treatment histories of the milder sex offenses that do exist, the results offer little that can be generalized to other offenders. Some have been cured, some not.

Therefore, to the question of whether or not treatment of sex offenders works, the reply must be that it never will until it is possible to study large groups of offenders, and try different treatment methods on them to determine what can be done in each type of case, and what new treatments can be applied to their problems—whatever those problems may be, which at this point is not known either.

Treatment of cancer in general doesn't work either. But in recent years, after massive amounts of research and experimentation, it is now clear that some types are treatable, some are operable, and some can be cured if caught in time. For the deadlier types, research continues in the hope that complete cures may still be found. We do not simply shrug and exclaim that it is untreatable simply because people are still dying of cancer. Instead, research for cures continues, financed by millions of dollars annually.

The same was true of polio a few years ago, and before that, tuberculosis, diphtheria, and smallpox. Only intensive research, such as was expended on these problems, will place the problem of the sex offender behind us, as treatment of these other diseases now is.

Therefore, what is necessary now is public support of treatment programs for sex offenders, and an openmindedness about what kinds of treatment modalities should be used. Certainly, everything that is available should be tried as long as the public has protection from the sex offender while these experimental treatments are being applied.

Centers for the treatment of sex offenders now exist in Bridgewater, Massachusetts; Rahway, New Jersey; Patuxent, Maryland; Fort Steilacoom, Washington, and a few other places in this country. They are mostly new. Some of them, most notably Fort Steilacoom, publish extensive reports on their treatment methods and their success rate.

A treatment rarely used in this country, but widely used in Europe, is castration. It is used in Denmark, Sweden, Norway, Germany, Holland, and Switzerland, and possibly also some of the other European countries. The above-named countries have all issued reports on the results of this treatment in recent years. References to these reports may be found in an extensive report on a thirty-year follow-up of castration cases in Denmark by Georg K. Stürup (in English), which is listed in the bibliography.

Castration is, and should be, used only as a treatment device, not a punishment procedure or a substitute for punishment. It is not the ghoulish horror that it may seem at first consideration. Nor does it necessarily remove a man's ability to engage in sexual intercourse. As explained

173

in the Stürup article, it is used in Denmark only at the request of the sex offender, and even then it is given careful consideration by a specially appointed board of examiners who attempt to determine whether or not the patient is likely to profit from the procedure.

It is not the same as sterilization, which simply results in a lack of fertility. In castration, the testes are removed. This ends the production of the androgens, which are the testicular hormones. However, the suprarenal male sexual hormones continue to be produced. Therefore, in many cases, sexual activity continues after castration, but at a reduced level.

The testes are replaced during the operation with prostheses consisting of small plastic balls inserted in the scrotum so that the man's outward appearance remains completely normal.

Denmark has been a pioneer in this treatment, and has had a castration law since 1929. This law provided for review of the results at a later date. Excellent records have been maintained since then, and thus it has been possible to conduct the long follow-up studies on each patient mentioned earlier.

Castration has been particularly successful and satisfactory to the men on whom it was performed, in those cases where an abnormally high sex drive was a matter of great distress and considerable abnormal behavior which resulted in the man's being incarcerated. In some of these cases, after a habitual erection and ejaculation rate of a dozen or more times a day, castration reduced the sexual activity of these men to three or four times a week. They were then able to take up normal lives, marry, and live successfully outside of the institution.

Obviously castration should be used only under the most carefully thought out conditions, and only in cases where both the sex offender and society might profit from the results. But it is a possible alternative to be considered along with all other treatment modalities such as behavior modification, psychodrama, group therapy, and any other developments that may come along.

Experimenting with any and all of these possibilities seems preferable to simply locking the sex offender away in a cell for life, or alternatively turning him out on the streets again when his propensity to rape is just as strong as when he was sentenced.

Also high on the priority list should be the development of methods which will enable us to determine at an early age, say ten or twelve years, whether or not a boy is headed in a direction that will make him a sex offender at twenty. But here again, it will be necessary to study large numbers of known sex offenders in order to discover what common patterns in their backgrounds existed at age twelve. At present there is no way to make this determination. Research on the sex offenders themselves and intensive study of their early history will be necessary to discover the key factors. Then these factors would have to be observed in young boys, and checked out as the boys grow older to determine which are the most important. Only then could we give tests to schoolchildren to find out which are headed for this kind of trouble, and determine what we can do to correct the problem in those who are.

In summary, it's time we started to look closely at rapists and all other sex offenders. The money, time, and effort now expended in attempting to help victims, increase police efforts, and institute new laws will only continue to increase unless we quickly invest some of it in finding out what is wrong with these individuals who cause the trouble with rape.

Bibliography

Sex Assault Bibliography
This bibliography is presented in two sections—One: General and Two: Child Molestation

Section One: General

Abdullah, Syed; Jarwik, Lissy F.; Kato, Takashi; Johnston, W. Cecil; Lanzkion, John. Extra Y Chromosomes and Its Psychiatric Implications. *Archives of General Psychiatry,* 21(4):497-501:1969.

Agopian, M.; Chappell, D.; Geis, G. Interracial Forcible Rape in a North American City: An Analysis of 63 Cases. In Drapkin, I. and Viano, E. (Eds.) *Victimology: A Reader.* Lexington, Mass.: Lexington Books, 1974.

Altman, Jack. *Born to Raise Hell.* New York: Grove Press, 1967.

Amir, Menachem. Forcible Rape. *Federal Probation,* 31:51-58:1967.

_____. Patterns in Forcible Rape: With Special Reference to Philadelphia, Pennsylvania, 1958-1960. Ann Arbor, Michigan: University Microfilms, 1965.

_____. Alcohol and Forcible Rape. *British Journal of Addiction,* 62:219:1967.

_____. Patterns in Forcible Rape. In Clinard, M. B. and Quinney, R. (Eds.) *Criminal Behavior Systems.* New York: Holt, 1967.

_____. *Patterns in Forcible Rape.* Chicago: University of Chicago Press, 1971.

_____. Victim Precipitated Forcible Rape. *Journal of Criminal Law,* 58:493:1967.

Anthony, F. W. Rape. *Boston Medical Surgical Journal,* 132:29:1895.

Bach-Y-Rita, George; Lion, John R.; Climent, Carlos E.; Ervin, Frank R. Episodic Dyscontrol: A Study of 130 Violent Patients. *American Journal of Psychiatry,* 127(11):1473-1478:1971.

Barber, Ross. An Investigation into Rape and Attempted

Rape Cases in Queensland. *Australia and New Zealand Journal of Criminology,* 6(4):214-217:Dec. 1973.

Barry, M. J. and Johnson, A. M. The Incest Barrier. *Psychoanalytic Quarterly,* 27:485:1958.

Bartholomew, A. A. A Long-Acting Phenothiazine as a Possible Agent to Control Deviant Sexual Behavior. *American Journal of Psychiatry,* 124:917:1968.

Beit-Hallahmi, Benjamin. Motivation for Murder: The Case of G. *Corrective Psychiatry and Journal of Social Therapy,* 17(1):25-30:1971.

Bernstein, Ellen and Rommel, Brandy. Rape. (Part II) Exploding the Myths. *Today's Health,* 53(9):36-39:1975.

Berschied, Ellen; Walster, Elaine; Barclay, Andrew. Effect of Time on Tendency to Compensate a Victim. *Psychological Reports,* 25(2):431-436:1969.

Bierer, J. and Somerer, G. A. Stilbestrol in Out-Patient Treatment of Sexual Offenders. *British Medical Journal,* 1:935:1950.

Blanchard, W. H. The Group Process in Gang Rape. *Journal of Social Psychology,* 49:259-266:1959.

Breen, James L.; Greenwald, Earl; Gregori, Caterina A. The Molested Young Female. *Pediatric Clinic of North America,* 19(3):717-725:1972.

Bremer, J. *Asexualization.* New York: Macmillan, 1959.

Bronson, R. F. False Accusations of Rape. *American Journal of Urology and Sexology.* 14:539-552:1918.

Brown, J. S. A Comparative Study of Deviations from Sexual Mores. *American Sociological Review,* 17:135: 1952.

Brownmiller, Susan. *Against Our Will.* New York: Simon and Schuster, 1975.

Burgess, Ann Walbert and Holmstrom, Lynda. *Rape: Victims of Crisis.* Englewood Cliffs, N.J.: Prentice-Hall, 1974.

Buss, A. H. *The Psychology of Aggression.* New York: John Wiley, 1961.

Calmas, Wilfred; Cohen, Murray; Seghorn, Theoharis. Sociometric Study of the Sex Offender. *Journal of Abnormal Psychology,* 74(2):249-255:1967.

Carlson, Kenneth A. Classes of Adult Offenders: A Multivariate Approach. *Journal of Abnormal Psychology,* 79(1):84-93:1972.

Chappell, Duncan; Geis, Gilbert; Schafer, Stephen; Siegal, Larry. Forcible Rape: A Comparative Study of Offenses Known to the Police in Boston and Los Angeles. In Henslin, J. M. *Sociology of Sex.* New York: Appleton Century Crofts, 1971.

Chappell, Duncan and Singer, Susan. Rape in New York City: A Study of Material in Police Files and Its Meaning. *Law and Society Review,* 1974.

Chatz, T. L. Recognizing and Treating Dangerous Sex Offenders. *International Journal of Offender Therapy and Comparative Criminology,* 16(2):116-120:1972.

Christensen, Anne-Lise and Nielsen, Johannes. Psychological Studies of Ten Patients with the XYY Syndrome. *British Journal of Psychiatry,* 123:219-221: 1973.

Clinch, Nancy Gager and Schurr, Cathleen. Rape. *The Washingtonian,* June 1973.

Cohen, Murray L.; Garofalo, Ralph; Boucher, Richard; Seghorn, Theoharis. The Psychology of Rapists. *Seminars in Psychiatry,* 3:307-327:1971.

Cohen, R. Sexual Molestations in Hospitals. *Clinical Pediatrics* (Philadelphia), 3:689:1964.

Cormier, Bruno M. and Simons, Siebert P. The Problem of the Dangerous Sexual Offender. *Canadian Psychiatric Association Journal,* 14(4):329-335:1969.

Cowan, H. Case of Rape During Sleep. *Edinburgh Medical Journal,* 8:570:1862.

Craig, R. *Sexual Psychopath Legislation: Task Force Report.* Submitted to the President's Commission on Law Enforcement and Administration of Justice. Washington, D.C., 1967.

Cuthbert, T. Martin. A Portfolio of Murder. *British Journal of Psychiatry,* 116:1-10:1969.

Davison, Gerald C. and Wilson, G. Terence. Goals and Strategies in Behavioral Treatment of Homosexual Pedophilia: Comments on a Case Study. *Journal of Abnormal Psychology,* 83(2):196-198:1974.

Doshay, L. J. *The Boy Offender and His Later Career.* New York: Grune, 1943.

Drzazga, John. *Sex Crimes,* Police Science Series. Chicago: Charles C. Thomas, 1960.

Erlanson, Otto. The Scene of a Sex Offense as Related to the Residence of the Offender. *Journal of Criminal Law,* 31:339-342:1940.

Ervard, John R. Rape, the Medical, Social, and Legal Implications. *American Journal of Obstetrics and Gynecology,* 111(1):497-499:1971.

Falk, Gerhard J. The Influence of the Seasons on Crime Rates. *Journal of Criminal Law, Criminology, and Police Science,* 43:199-213:1952.

Ferracuti, F. and Wolfgang, M. E. A Design for a Proposed Study of Violence. *British Journal of Criminology,* 3:377-388:1963.

Fitch, J. H. Men Convicted of Sexual Offenses against Children. *British Journal of Criminology,* 3:18-31:1962.

Forbes, Gilbert. Sexual Offenses. *The Practitioner,* 209:287-293:1972.

Fox, Sandra Sutherland and Scherl, Donald J. Crisis Intervention with Victims of Rape. *Social Work,* 37-42: January 1972.

Frank, G. *The Boston Strangler.* New York: New American Library, 1966.

Gagnon, John H. and Simon, William. Sexual Encounters between Adults and Children. *Sex Information and Education Council of the United States,* Study Guide GII, 1853 Broadway, New York, New York 10023.

Gebhard, Paul; Gagnon, John H.; Wardell, B.; and Christenson, Cornelia V. *Sex Offenders: An Analysis of Types.* New York: Harper and Row, 1965.

Geis, Gilbert and Chappell, Duncan. Forcible Rape by

Multiple Offenders. *Abstracts of Criminology and Penology,* 4:431-436:1971.

Geis, Gilbert. Group Sexual Assaults. *Medical Aspects of Human Sexuality,* 5:100-113:May 1971.

Giacinti, Thomas A. and Tjaden, Claus. *The Crime of Rape in Denver.* Denver Anti-Crime Council, 1313 Tremont Place, Suite 5, Denver, Colorado.

Glueck, B. C. Final Report Research for the Study and Treatment of Persons Convicted of Crimes Involving Sexual Aberrations. New York: State Department of Hygiene, 1956.

Goldhirsh, Mark L. Manifest Content of Dreams of Convicted Sex Offenders. *Journal of Abnormal and Social Psychology,* 63(3):643-645:1961.

Goldstein, Michael J. and Kant, Harold S. with Hartman, John J. *Pornography and Sexual Deviance.* Berkeley, Calif.: University of California Press, 1973.

Guttmacher, M. S. *Sex Offenses: The Problem, Causes, and Prevention.* New York: Norton, 1951.

Hackett, Thomas P. The Psychotherapy of Exhibitionists in a Court Clinic Setting. *Seminars in Psychiatry.* 3(3):297-306:1971.

Halleck, Seymour L. The Physician's Role in Management of Victims of Sex Offenders. *Journal of the American Medical Association,* 180(4):273-278:1962.

Harrison, M. J. G. and Tennet, T. G. Neurological Anomalies in XYY Males. *British Journal of Psychiatry,* 120:447:1972.

Hayman, C. R. Lanza, Charlene. Sexual Assault on Women and Girls. *American Journal of Obstetrics and Gynecology.* 109(1):480-86:1971.

Hayman, Charles R.; Lewis, Francis R.; Stewart, William F.; Grant, Murray. A Public Health Program for Sexually Assaulted Females. *Public Health Reports,* 82(6):497-504:1967.

Hayman, C. R. (Editorial). Sexual Assault on Women and Girls. *Annals of Internal Medicine,* 72(2):277-278:1970.

181

———. Sexual Assault on Women and Girls in the District of Columbia. *Southern Medical Journal,* 62:1227:1969.

Hook, Ernest B. Behavioral Implications of the Human XYY Genotype. *Science,* 179:139-150:1973.

Howard, J. C. *Administration of Rape Cases in the City of Baltimore and the State of Maryland.* Baltimore, Maryland: Monumental Bar Association, 1967.

Howell, Leisla M. Clinical and Research Impressions Regarding Murder and Sexually Perverse Crimes. *Psychotherapy and Psychosomatics,* 21:156-159:1972.

Johnson, A. M. and Robinson, D. B. The Sexual Deviant (Sexual Psychopath)—Causes, Treatment, and Prevention. *Journal of the American Medical Association,* 164:1559:1957.

Johnson, John. Psychopathia Sexualis. *British Journal of Psychiatry,* 122:211-218:1973.

Jones, Cathaleene and Aronson, Elliott. Attribution of Fault to a Rape Victim as a Function of Respectability of the Victim. *Journal of Personality and Social Psychology,* 26(3):415-419:1973.

Justice, Blaire and Birkman, Roger. An Effort to Distinguish the Violent from the Non-Violent. *Southern Medical Journal,* 65(1):704-706:1972.

Kaplan, Helen S. *The New Sex Therapy.* New York: New York Times Book Co., 1974.

Karacan, I.; Hursch, C. J.; Guerrero, M. W.; Williams, R. L. The Nocturnal Penile Tumescence of Convicted Rapists and Other Prisoners. *Sleep Research,* 1: 61:1972.

Karpman, B. *The Sexual Offender and His Offenses.* New York: Julian, 1954.

Kercher, Glen A. and Walker, C. Eugene. Reactions of Convicted Rapists to Sexually Explicit Stimuli. *Journal of Abnormal Psychology,* 81(1):46-50:1973.

Kohlenberg, Robert J. Case Report: Treatment of a Homosexual Pedophiliac Using In Vivo Desensitization: A Case Study. *Journal of Abnormal Psychology,* 83 (2): 192-195:1974.

Kolarsky, Alex and Madlafousek, Jaroslav. Female Behavior and Sexual Arousal in Heterosexual Male Deviant Offenders. *Journal of Nervous and Mental Disease,* 155(2):110-118:1972.

Kozol, Harry L. The Diagnosis and Treatment of Dangerousness. *Crime and Delinquency,* 371-392: October 1972.

_____. Myths about the Sex Offender. *Medical Aspects of Human Sexuality,* 5(6):50-62:1971.

Krafft-Ebing, R. *Psychopathia Sexualis.* Chicago: W. T. Keener, 1900.

Kraus, J. Trends in the Rates of Murder, Manslaughter and Rape among Male Juveniles (N.S.W. 1956-69). *Australia and New Zealand Journal of Criminology,* 5(3):146-156:Sept. 1972.

Kutner, S. Jerome. Sex Guilt and the Sexual Behavior Sequence. *Journal of Sex Research,* 7(2):107-115:1971.

Leppman, F. Essential Differences between Sex Offenders. *Journal of Criminal Law,* 32:366:1941.

Lustig, M. et. al. Incest. *Archives of General Psychiatry* (Chicago), 14:31:1966.

LeVine, R. A. Gusii Sex Offenses: A Study in Social Control. *American Anthropology.* 61:965:1959.

MacDonald, George J. and Williams, Robinson A. Characteristics and Management of Committed Sexual Offenders in the State of Washington. *State of Washington,* Fort Steilacoom, Washington, January, 1971.

_____. Community Adjustment of Treated Sexual Offenders. *State of Washington,* Fort Steilacoom, Washington, January, 1971.

_____. The Washington State Sexual Psychopath Law, A Review of Twenty Years' Experience. *State of Washington,* Fort Steilacoom, Washington, January, 1971.

MacDonald, John M. *Rape: Offenders and Their Victims.* Springfield, Ill.: Charles C. Thomas, 1971.

McCord, W. and McCord, P. V. Family Relationships and Sexual Deviance in Lower-Class Adolescents. *International Journal of Social Psychiatry,* 8:165-180: 1962.

McCaldon, R. J. Rape. *Canadian Journal of Correction,* 9:37-59:1967.

Malinowski, B. *The Sexual Life of Savages in Northwestern Melanesia.* New York: Eugenica, 1929.

Massey, Joe B.; Garcia, Celso-Ramon; and Emich, John P., Jr. Management of Sexually Assaulted Females. *Journal of Obstetrics and Gynecology,* 38(1):29-36: 1971.

Matza, D. *Becoming Deviant.* Englewood Cliffs, N.J.: Prentice-Hall, 1969.

Masters, W. H. and Johnson, V. E. *Human Sexual Inadequacy.* Boston: Little, 1970.

Milliken, Rhoda. The Sex Offender's Victim. *Federal Probation,* 14(3):22-26:1950.

Medea, A. and Thompson, K. *Against Rape.* New York. Farrar, Straus, and Giroux. 1974.

Meyer, Timothy P. The Effect of Sexually Arousing and Violent Films on Aggressive Behavior. *Journal of Sex Research,* 8(4):324-331:1962.

Mohr, J. W. A Follow-up Study of Sexual Offenders. *Forensic Clinic,* Clarke Institute, Ottawa:1960-1961.

————. A Short Survey of Sexual Offenders in Ontario Reformatory, Millbrook. *Canada Journal of Correction,* 5:229-235:1963.

————. Rape and Attempted Rape. Mimeographed. Toronto: Toronto Psychiatric Hospital, October 1965.

Mueller, G. O. Legal Regulation of Sexual Conduct. New York: Oceana, 1961.

Northwestern University School of Law. Complainant Credibility in Sexual Offense Cases: A Survey of Character Testimony and Psychiatric Experts. *Journal of Criminal Law and Criminology,* 64(1):67-75:1973.

Palm, R. and Abrahamsen, D. A Rorschach Study of the Wives of Sex Offenders. *Journal of Nervous and Mental Diseases,* 119:167:1954.

Parker, Tony. *The Twisting Lane: The Hidden World of Sex Offenders.* New York: Harper and Row, 1972.

Pasco, H. Deviate Sexual Behavior and the Sex Criminal. *Canadian Medical Association Journal,* 84:206-211:1961.

Perdue, William C. and Lester, David. Personality Characteristics of Rapists. *Perceptual and Motor Skills,* 35:514:1972.

Perr, I. N. Statutory Rape of an Insane Person. *Journal of Forensic Science.* 13:433:1968.

Peters, Joseph J.; Pedigo, James M.; Steg, Joseph; McKenna, James J. Group Psychotherapy of the Sex Offender. *Federal Probation,* September 1968.

Ploscowe, M. *Sex and the Law.* Englewood Cliffs, N.J.: Prentice-Hall, 1951.

Popella, E. Uber Delikt-fordernde Situationengund ihr Beurteilung bei Sexualvergehen Jugendlucher (The Crime-encouraging Situation and Its Influence in Juvenile Sexual Offenses). *Nervenarzt,* Jena, E. Germany, 39(2):67-70:1968.

Rabach, J. and Nedoma, K. Indications of Testicular Pulpectomy in Sexual Delinquents. *Ceskoslovenska Psychiatrie,* 66(3):152-157:1970.

Radzinowicz, L. *Sexual Offenses.* London: Macmillan, 1957.

Raphling, David; Carpenter, Bob; Davis, Allan. Incest, A Geneological Study. *Archives of General Psychiatry,* 16:505-511:April 1967.

Rentzel, Lance. *When All the Laughter Died in Sorrow.* New York: Saturday Review Press, 1972.

Reifen, David. The Sex Offender and His Victim. *International Child Welfare Review,* 12:109-124:1958.

Reinhardt, J. M. *Sex Perversions and Sex Crimes.* Springfield, Ill.: Charles C. Thomas, 1957.

Riemer, S. A Research Note on Incest. *American Journal of Sociology,* 45:566:1939.

Roberts, Robert E.; Abrams, Laurence; Finch, John R. "Delinquent" Sexual Behavior among Adolescents. *Medical Aspects of Human Sexuality,* 7(1):162-183:1973.

Rooth, Graham. Exhibitionism, Sexual Violence, and Pedophilia. *British Journal of Psychiatry,* 122:705-710:1973.

Rupp, Joseph C. Sperm Survival and Prostatic Acid Phosphatase Activity in Victims of Sexual Assault. *Journal of Forensic Sciences,* 14:177-183:1969.

Russell, Diana E. H. *The Politics of Rape.* New York: Stein and Day, 1975.

Sadoff, Robert L. Anonymous Sexual Offenders. *Medical Aspects of Human Sexuality,* 6(3):118-123:1972.

Sagarin, Edward and MacNamara, Donald E. *Problems of Sex Behavior.* New York: Thomas Y. Crowell, 1968.

Schafer, S. *The Victim and His Criminal: A Study in Functional Responsibility.* New York: Random House, 1968.

Schafer, S. and Geis, G. Forcible Rape: A Comparative Study of Offenses Known to the Police in Boston and Los Angeles, 1967. A paper presented at the Annual Meeting of the American Sociological Association, September 1969.

Schapper, Beatrice. What We Now Know About Sex Molesters. *Today's Health,* January 1966.

Schiff, A. F. Rape in Other Countries. *Medical Science Law,* 11:139-143:1971.

―――. Rape. *Medical Aspects of Human Sexuality,* 76-84, May 1972.

―――. Statistical Features of Rape. *Journal of Forensic Sciences,* 14:102-110:1969.

―――. Rape in Foreign Countries. *Medical Trial Technique Quarterly,* 120:66-74:1973.

Schonfelder, Thea. Sexual Traumata in der Kindheit und ihre Folgen (Sexual Trauma in Childhood and Its Consequences). *Praxis der Psychotherapie,* 15(1):12-20:1970.

Schultz, Leroy G. Interviewing the Sex Offender's Victim. *Journal of Criminal Law, Criminology and Police Science,* 50:448-452:1960.

Schurr, Cathleen. Rape Victim as Criminal. Reprinted in 1972 by Know, Inc., P.O. Box 86031, Pittsburgh, Pennsylvania 15021.

Schwartz, Barry. The Effect in Philadelphia of Pennsylvania's Increased Penalties for Rape and Attempted Rape. *Journal of Criminal Law, Criminology and Police Science,* 59(4):509-515:1968.

See, Carolyn. Rape (Part I) No Woman Is Immune. *Today's Health,* 53(9):30-35:1975.

Shaffer, Helen B. Crime of Rape. *Editorial Research Reports,* 1:41-69:1972.

Sharpe, N. The Significance of Spermatozoa in Victims of Sexual Offenses. *Canadian Medical Association Journal,* 89:513:1963.

Sidley, Nathan and Stolarz, Frances J. A Proposed "Dangerous Sex Offender" Law. *American Journal of Psychiatry,* 130 (7):765-768:1973.

Sloane, P. and Karpinski, E. Effects of Incest on the Participants. *American Journal of Orthopsychiatry,* 12:666:1942.

Slovenko, R. *Sexual Behavior and the Law.* Springfield, Ill.: Charles C. Thomas, 1965.

Smith, Sir Sidney. Refresher Course for General Practitioners—Alleged Rape. *British Medical Journal,* 2:1454-1457:1951.

Spencer, J. C. Contribution to the Symposium on Sexual Deviation. *Canada Journal of Correction,* 3:481-485:1961.

Stürup, George K. Treatment of Sexual Offenders in Herstedvester Denmark. *Acta Psychiatrica Scandinavica,* Supplementum 204, 44:5-61:1968.

Sutherland, Sandra and Scherl, Donald J. Patterns of Response among Victims of Rape. *American Journal of Orthopsychiatry,* 40(3):503-511:1970.

Svalastoga, Kaare. Rape and Social Structure. *Pacific Sociological Review,* 5:48053:1962.

Thoinot, L. and Weysse, A. M. *Medicolegal Aspects of Moral Offenses.* Philadelphia: Davis, 1921.

Verocolo, Alfred B. *The Repetitive Sex Offender.* Roselle, N.J.: Quality Printing, 1969.

Wambaugh, Joseph. *The Onion Field.* New York: Dell Publishing Co., 1974.

Warder, J. Two Studies of Violent Offenders. *British Journal of Criminology,* 9(4):389-393:1969.

Watsa, M. C. Rape. *Indian Journal of Medical Science,* 16:366:1962.

Weinburg, S. K. *Incest Behavior.* New York: Citadel, 1955.

Weiner, I. B. On Incest: A Survey. *Excerpta Criminologia,* 4:137:1964.

Weiss, Joseph; Roger, Estelle; Darwin, Miriam R.; Dutton, Charles E. A Study of Girl Sex Victims. *Psychiatric Quarterly,* 29:1-26:1955.

Wells, Nesta. Sexual Offenses as Seen by a Woman Police Surgeon. *British Medical Journal,* 2:1404-1408:1958.

Werner, Arnold. Rape: Interruption of the Therapeutic Process by External Stress. *Psychotherapy: Theory, Research and Practice,* 9(4):349-351:1972.

Wile, W. F. Case Study of a Rapist: An Analysis of the Causation of Criminal Behavior. *Journal of Social Therapy,* 7:10-21:1961.

Williams, Arthur Hyatt. Rape-Murder. *Sexual Behavior and the Law.* Springfield, Ill.: Charles C. Thomas, 1965.

Williams, Cindy Cook and Williams, Reg Arthur. Rape: A Plea for Help in the Emergency Room. *Nursing Forum,* 21(4):388-401:1973

Williams, Ruth. *Cry Rape.* New York. Universal Publishing and Distributing Corp., 1974.

Wortis, Joseph. Sex Taboos, Sex Offenders, and the Law. *American Journal of Orthopsychiatry,* 9:554-564:1939.

Zechnich, Robert. Exhibitionism: Genesis, Dynamics and Treatment. *Psychiatric Quarterly,* 45(1):70-75:1971.

Section Two: Child Molestation

Bender, Lauretta and Blau, Abraham. The Reaction of Children to Sexual Relations with Adults. *American Journal of Orthopsychiatry,* 7:500-518:1937.

Bender, Lauretta and Grugett, Alvin E., Jr. A Follow-up Report on Children Who Had Atypical Sexual Experience. *American Journal of Orthopsychiatry,* 22:825-837:1952.

Bryce, C. A. A Boy of Seven Raped by a Nymphomaniac, and Infected with Syphilis. *Southern Clinician,* 4:159:1881.

Cavallin, H. Incestuous Fathers: A Clinical Report. *American Journal of Psychiatry,* 122:1132:1966.

Chaneles, Sol. Child Victims of Sexual Offenders. *Federal Probation,* 52-56:Sept. 1950.

Cormier, B. M. et al. Psychodynamics of Father-Daughter Incest. *Canadian Psychiatric Association Journal,* 7:203:1962.

De Francis, Vincent. Protecting the Child Victim of Sex Crimes. *American Humane Association,* Children's Division, May 1965.

Eaton, A. P. The Sexually Molested Child. *Clinical Pediatrics,* Phila., 8:438:1969.

Gagnon, John H. Female Child Victims of Sex Offenses. *Social Problems,* 13:176-192:1965.

Gibbens, T. C. N. Child Victims of Sex Offenses. *Institute for the Study and Treatment of Delinquency.* London, England: 1963.

Henriques, Sir Basil. Sex Assaults on Children, A Magistrate's View. *British Medical Journal,* 2:1628-1633:1961.

Kaufman, Irving; Peck, Alice L.; Taguiri, Consuelo K. The Family Constellation and Overt Incestuous Relations between Father and Daughter. *American Journal of Orthopsychiatry,* 24:266-279:1954.

Koupernik, C.; Masciangelo, P. M.; Balestra-Beretta, S. A Case of Heller's Dementia Following Sexual Assault on a Four-Year-Old Girl. *Child Psychiatry and Human Development,* 2(3):134-144:1972.

Landis, Judson T. Experiences of 500 Children with Adult Sexual Deviation. *Psychiatric Quarterly Supplement,* 30:91-109:1956.

Lewis, Melvin and Sarrel, Philip. Some Psychological Aspects of Seduction, Incest and Rape and Childhood. *Journal of American Academy of Child Psychiatry,* 8(2)606-619:1969.

Lipton, G. L. and Roth, E. J. Rape: A Complex Management Problem in the Pediatric Emergency Room. *Journal of Pediatrics,* 75(5):859-866:1969.

Litin, E. M. et al. Parental Influence in Unusual Sexual Behavior in Children. *Psychoanalytic Quarterly,* 25:37:1956.

McGeorge, J. Sexual Assaults on Children. *Medical Science and Law,* 4:245:1964.

Medlicott, R. W. Lot and His Daughters—Parent-Child Incest in the Bible and Mythology. *Australia and New Zealand Journal of Psychiatry,* 1:134:1967.

——— Parent-Child Incest. *Australia and New Zealand Journal of Psychiatry,* 1:134:1967.

Messer, A. A. The Phaedra Complex. *Archives of General Psychiatry* (Chicago), 21:213:1969.

Middleton, R. Brother-Sister and Father-Daughter Marriage in Ancient Egypt. *American Sociological Review,* 27:603:1962.

Mohr, J. W.; Turner, R. E., Jerry, M. B. *Pedophilia and Exhibitionism.* Toronto: University of Toronto Press, 1965.

Oliven, John F. *Sexual Hygiene and Pathology. A Manual for the Physician and the Professions. Second Edition. Ch. IV. The Child as Victim of Sexual Aggression.* Philadelphia. Pa.: J. P. Lippincott Co., 1965. Pp. 55-71.

Peters, Joseph J. Child Rape: Defusing a Psychological Time Bomb. *Hospital Physician,* 46-49:Feb. 1973.

Peters, Joseph J. and Resnik, H. L. Probationed Paedophiles: Treatment Results with Out-Patient Group Psychotherapy. *Excerpta Medica International Congress Series No. 150.* Proceedings of the IV World Congress of Psychiatry, Madrid, 5-11 September 1966. Pp. 3073-3076.

Reifen, David. Protection of Children Involved in Sexual Offenses: A New Method of Investigation in Israel. *Journal of Criminal Law, Criminology and Police Science,* 49:222-229:1958.

Revitch, E. and Weiss, R. The Pedophilia Offender. *Disease and Nervous System,* 27:37-78:1962.

Rogers, Estelle and Weiss, Joseph. *Study of Sex Crimes against Children—Introduction and Conclusions.* Langley Porter Clinic, San Francisco, 1953.

Schultz, Leroy G. The Child Sex Victim: Social, Psychological, and Legal Perspectives. *Child Welfare,* 52(3)147-157:1972.

Shopper, Moisy. Psychiatric and Legal Aspects of Statutory Rape, Pregnancy, and Abortion in Juveniles. *Journal of Psychiatry and Law,* 1(3):275-295:1973.

Tormes, Y. M. Child Victims of Incest. Denver: *American Humane Association,* n.d.

Wahl, C. W. The Psychodynamics of Consummated Maternal Incest. *Archives of General Psychiatry* (Chicago), 3:88:1960.

Walker, J. Reports, with Comments, of Twenty-one Cases of Indecent Assault and Rape upon Children. *Archives of Pediatrics,* 3:269:1886.

Weiner, I. R. Father-Daughter Incest: A Clinical Report. *Psychiatric Quarterly,* 36:607:1962.

Wells, Nesta. Sex Assaults on Children, Medical Aspects. *British Medical Journal,* 2:1628-1633:1961.

Williams, G. Rape in Children and Young Girls. *International Clinician,* 2:245:1913.

Index

Index